PRAISE FOR

Great Faith

Great faith is my greatest goal and I am sure it is yours also. How do I attain great faith? By reading God's Word, hanging around God's great faith people and reading great faith books. This is why I really received from Pastor Wendell Smith's book. I want to keep casting my net on the other side. I want to keep increasing in faith - not shrinking. I really like what he states about shrinking faith. Wow, do I ever need to be sensitive to do the "ridiculous" when He is leading me to do so. This book will help you not to give in, give up, or give out!

MARILYN HICKEY
President, Marilyn Hickey Ministries

Taking a Church from the beginning with few people – and bringing it to a place of world renown is difficult, but Wendell Smith almost makes it look easy. When you look deeper, you can feel his pain, frustration and momentary fear – and then see his faith in action!

This book is going to be a great help to Ministers, Pastors and people. It is going to challenge those with a real call to raise up a local Church, to rise up, get direction from God, pray, cry at times – but have faith and do it!

Those who are just looking for a job and a paycheck, will stay at home and do something else. And this is good. Well done, Wendell and Gini Smith.

PASTOR CHARLES GREEN
Faith Church, New Orleans, LA

It is obvious that Wendell Smith has had an experience with God! His book, Great Faith *is a must read for anyone that needs a path to follow from the natural to the supernatural. He has successfully crafted a map that if applied to our daily walk, will link our humanity with His divinity. Great faith is the key!*

TOMMY TENNEY

Great Faith *is written out of great faith experiences of Wendell and Gini Smith. This book will be an inspiration to all who need a lifting of vision, a new spirit of adventure, a reminder of how big our God is and will bring encouragement to every person who desires to move from little faith to great faith.*

FRANK DAMAZIO
Senior Pastor, City Bible Church

It has been my privilege to know and work with Wendell Smith for nearly 30 years. From the time we met it was evident that the hand of God was upon him. As I reflect back on our years of working together in Bible Temple (now City Bible Church) it is easy to understand why this book has been written. Wendell and Gini have always been people of faith. They have always had great trust in the Lord. Their vision and goals always have been clear, but larger than life. The truths of this book express the heart of Wendell and Gini. With God, they really believe, nothing is impossible!

DICK IVERSON
Chairman, Ministers Fellowship International

Wendell Smith is a leader whose ministry is touching thousands of people. This book will be a very practical guide of how one leader has been used of the Lord and how readers can gain first hand guidance and direction and see the same things happen in their ministry or place of leadership. This book is a must read for pastors who want to impact their community!

DON ARGUE, ED. D.
President, Northwest College
Kirkland, WA

Wendell Smith is what the writer of Hebrews encourages us to be: "Imitators of those who through faith and patience inherit the promises." Derek Prince once said: "All progress in the Chrisitian life is by faith." I am convinced that the substance of Wendell's life message is exactly that. What Wendell shares is straight from life; no hype – just raw faith. That faith has propelled Wendell Smith, The City Church, and those who touch his sphere into incredible opportunities and blessings. Wendell and Gini Smith have demonstrated the possibilities that become realities when your life and vision is marked by Credendo Vides: *"By believing, one sees." Don't just read this book; but rather drink deeply of its message.*

BISHOP JOSEPH L. GARLINGTON
Senior Pastor, Covenant Church of Pittsburgh

How refreshing to have a new, wonderful book on the subject of faith! It is like a fresh breeze of the Holy Spirit filling up our sails. I know Wendell Smith and I have been to his church. I have seen first hand the work of faith on his life. I think this is the right time for such a book. May this volume be a blessing and inspiration to every person who reads it, so we can do exploits for His kingdom.

HAROLD CABALLEROS
Senior Pastor, El Shaddai Church
Member, Church Growth International Board

Anyone can write about faith, but only those who have experienced it can mentor others. Whether you're looking for immediate help or for lasting improvement in life, this book is pure gold.

BOB HARRISON
President, Christian Business Leaders International

I highly endorse my dear friend Wendell Smith's book, Great Faith. *Through this book, God has released supernatural faith in these last days so that we can fulfill the incredible destiny that is on our lives in the Body of Christ. Wendell's book releases into your life the gift of faith that will move the mountains and bring the Kingdom of God on earth as it is in heaven. How happy the heart of the Lord must be as Great Faith is stirred in the heart of believers world-wide through this book.*

BOB WEINER

Over the past few years my faith has been stirred more than I ever could have imagined by the simple yet profound example and teaching of a very close friend, Wendell Smith. Having known him all of his life I have been able to observe the work of God in and through his life. This book details his life message of faith. It is indeed the way he lives and the way he walks out his life in Christ. It comes from the experience of being a pastor, a leader, a husband, and a father. This book will change you and your ministry as you read it with a spirit of expectation. It has changed me. The life of faith that is spoken of in this book will bring about dramatic transformations in your life. The Body of Christ needs this message if it is to move into the next level of spiritual maturity. It is a must read for every believer.

KEN WILDE
Senior Pastor, Capital Christian Center

Wendell's book on Great Faith *is bound to be a blesssing and encouragement to all. Wendell is 'out there', far ahead as a leader, an entrepreneur and a man of 'great faith'. As Wendell was asked the question, "Are you a faith preacher?", he truly answered, "I am not an unbelief preacher!" There is a certain amount of 'faith preaching' that is not truly Biblical, but Wendell, in his book, takes us back to the true source of faith - that is JESUS himself, the author and finisher of our faith! May Wendell's book be a strength to all who read it.*

KEVIN CONNER
Waverley Christian Fellowship
Melbourne, Australia

Great Faith *is not just great stories; it is a greater understanding of faith, greater inspiration to visualize God's plan, and greater equipping to put the tools of faith into action. Pastor Wendell will impassion you in your pursuit of faith. Are you ready to be catapulted into the exponential rewards of great faith?*

PASTOR BENNY PEREZ
Founder and Executive Director, Pacesetters International

This book is more than an intellectual treatise on faith. It comes out of the heart of a man of God, a man of integrity. The truth of this book was birthed by revelation to Pastor Smith several years ago as he diligently studied God's financial plan for the believer.

Having served with Pastor Smith for 8 years, I emphatically declare that he has practiced what he preaches! His amazing steps of faith on many occasions have modeled that faith as a lifestyle. I have seen the supernatural provision for City Church in Kirkland, WA as we have followed Pastor's leadership in obedience and faith.

This book releases new confidence in God. It renews our understanding of the goodness of God. It opens new facets of truth, enlarging our vision and faith. The reader will surely be encouraged to accept the Bible verse, "Our God is able to do exceedingly abundantly above all that we can ask or imagine!"

DON OSTROM
Elder, The City Church

My warm, personal friend and brother, Pastor Wendell Smith, has given us an amazing book, one I treasure to read and study and apply many new thoughts about faith to my own life and ministry.

In preaching in his great Bible church I've seen where he has led the people from almost point zero to a living, Spirit-filled, signs and wonders church where people come with their struggles and find deliverance.

My whole life and ministry is consumed by living by faith. My faith in our risen Christ has produced everything I've been enabled by the Holy Spirit to accomplish. I'm always looking for better ways to release my faith and Wendell has mightily helped me.

I promise you if you even read a portion of this book your faith will rise to a new high. Be sure and get your own personal copy. You'll renew your faith and mount up with wings as eagles!

DR. ORAL ROBERTS

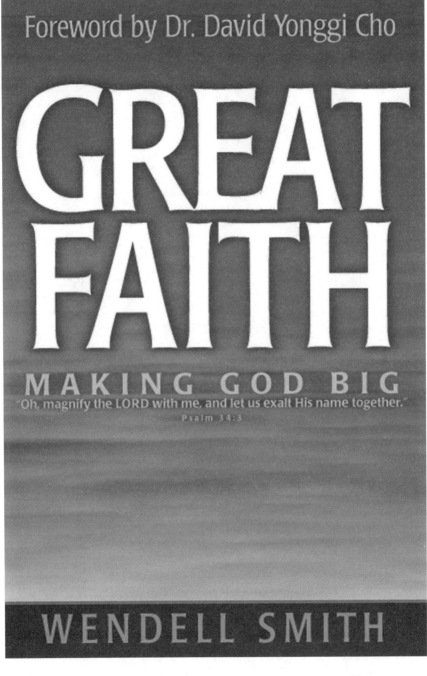

Foreword by Dr. David Yonggi Cho

GREAT FAITH

MAKING GOD BIG

"Oh, magnify the LORD with me, and let us exalt His name together."
Psalm 34:3

WENDELL SMITH

CityChristianPublishing
www.CityChristianPublishing.com

Published by City Christian Publishing
9200 NE Fremont
Portland, Oregon 97220

Printed in U.S.A.

Great Faith
© Copyright 2001 by Wendell Smith
All Rights Reserved

ISBN: 1-886849-79-X
ISBN13: 978-1-886849-79-2

City Christian Publishing is a ministry of City Bible Church and is dedicated to serving the local church and its leaders through the production and distribution of quality restoration materials. It is our prayer that these materials, proven in the context of the local church, will equip leaders in exalting the Lord and extending His kingdom.

For a free catalog of additional resources from City Christian Publishing please call 1-800-777-6057 or visit our web site at www.citychristianpublishing.com.

Library of Congress Cataloging-in-Publication Data

Smith, Wendell, 1950-
Great faith : making God big / Wendell Smith.
    p. cm.
ISBN 1-886849-79-X (alk. paper)
    1. Faith.   I. Title.
    BV4637 .S5577 2001
    234'.23--dc21

                            2001001908

To our Pastors Dick & Edie Iverson
– President and Founder of Minister Fellowship International

Brother Dick and Edie, Gini and I want to thank you for your love for us and for your faithful and loyal support of our pioneering years here in Seattle. This book is a reflection of your faith and your input into our hearts and lives for so many years. We could not have had the success we have had without you and the faith-filled foundation that you laid in our lives. Our children are your grandchildren in the Lord. And this story of our journey of faith is part of your reward and inheritance as well.

To Don and Marlene Ostrom
– Elders of The City Church, Seattle

Don, your faith and friendship has been one of the most special treasures of pastoring over these past eight years. I am not sure we could have accomplished what we did without you and Marlene. Your example in the realms of faith spurred us on many times and gave us the extra boost we needed to continue our walk of faith. This book is not just my journey of faith but yours as well. I thank you for believing in your Pastor.

Marlene, you have equally encouraged and blessed Gini and I over these past many years. So many times, your joy (living up to your name) and your encouragement meant the world to us and helped us make it through a difficult time. Thank you for your sweetness and faithfulness and for helping us build great faith into our beautiful congregation.

To Ken and Connie Wilde
– Pastors, Capitol Christian Center, Boise Idaho

Ken, no one but Gini has helped me more than you have during our eight years of pioneering. Your confidence, covering and love has helped me so many times, I have lost count. You are a friend that sticks closer than a brother and so faithful and loyal to us. I am not sure we could have made it without you and Connie. We love you with all our hearts and thank God for your faith in us and in what the Lord was doing in our lives.

To Wendy and Benny and BJ Perez
– Pacesetters International

Wendy, I want to thank you for your special place in our lives. You are our firstborn and very holy unto the Lord. No one can ever take your place. But your spirit and love for the Lord, for people, for us, for your husband, and now for your firstborn makes us proud to say that you are our daughter. The stories and faith I describe in this book are a reflection of many people, but none more important than you. Your personal faith has been an inspiration to me as your father. I love you with all my heart and thank you for honoring me and walking in truth. Always walk with God, baby, and you will be blessed and favored.

Benny, thank you for being the man of God you are. And thank you for loving Wendy as much as you do. We have been blessed to have you become part of our family and life. We so greatly admire your passion and love and zeal, but especially your faith. Your life has become part of the fabric of our lives and our faith. We are blessed every time we watch you minister to people and allow the Holy Spirit to pour through you. I am blessed to be your father in law and I love you very much.

BJ, Your grandpa and grandma love you so much. You are one of the greatest joys of our lives. The grace and anointing of God will always be on your life and you are destined to do many great things for the Name of the Lord. Someday, your Daddy and your Mommy will read this book about faith to you and tell you of the wonderful things God did for all of us. And He will do great things for you too! "You are so beautiful to me!" I love you big boy!

To Judah and Chelsea Smith

Judah, I want to thank you for making me so proud to be a father. You are a son indeed, and not only mine, but also His. Your passion and zeal for the things of God has been unrivaled among your peers. And your faith is a great inspiration to so many and a part of our story in being able to walk in faith before my generation. I want to thank you for following the Lord with all your heart and being such a pristine model for others to pattern their lives after. My prayer is that the principles in this book will be part of your inheritance as well and you will walk it out in front of your generation and beyond. I love you my son. Always be strong in the grace that is in Christ Jesus.

Chelsea, you are a great joy to our hearts. We have been so blessed to have you become part of our lives and family. You were definitely destined to marry Judah. Thank you, honey, for loving him so much and for loving the Lord too. You and your family are part of this story and a wonderful chapter in our journey of faith. I love you with all my heart and thank you for walking in a way that is so pleasing to the Lord, honoring of your parents, and influential among your peers. May you always have great faith to face your bright future with Judah.

To Yvonne Hernandez

Mom, this book would not be going to print without you. Thank you for praying for Gini and listening to the voice of the Holy Spirit back in 1971 to send her back to school, so we could meet. Thank you for praying for her husband before you knew me. And thank you for being a woman of great faith yourself in following the Lord all these years and influencing all our lives in the ways of godliness. You are a very special part of this book and the story of our journey of faith. I love you with all my heart and thank you for loving me and believing in me for 29 years.

To Woody and Dorothy Smith

Mom, there would be no Great Faith book without you. (Tim and Chris and I all thank you for not stopping after Terry and Steve!) Thank you for raising me in the fear and admonition of the Lord. Thank you for your amazing faithfulness to the Lord over many years of valleys and mountain peaks. Raising the five of us took great faith for sure. But your faith and love for the Lord, your love for the Lord's Church, the way you have always honored Dad, and the way you have faithfully loved each of your children and grandchildren through the good times and bad is a testimony to a woman of virtue and life lived with true and sincere faith. Such is my foundation. This woman is my mother. I am a son that has received great blessing. I love you, Mom.

Dad, although you are not here on earth with us at this time, I want to write down my expression of thanks to you for giving me life and leading me to new life in Jesus Christ. I believe that your mantle for church growth, for preaching and your passion for souls has been passed down to me. Gini and I have picked up your torch and the hundreds of souls we care for today are a reflection of the unfinished foundation you worked on in pioneering churches in this region, and of the foundation of faith you laid in my life so many years ago. I love you and look forward to our reunion in Heaven and being able to tell you all our stories of faith firsthand!

To Virginia Renee Smith

And especially to my dear wife I dedicate this book. Gin, I could never thank you with enough words to express my appreciation for what you have done in helping your husband finish this book. Besides, I have used up all the words in my thesaurus. But how about a few like, "fabulous, remarkable, extraordinary, astonishing, astounding, marvelous, surpassing, spectacular, splendid, incomparable, and rare?" You are the best. I truly owe my greatest debt of gratitude to you, not just because you edited and re-read this text so many times, but because you are Sister Wisdom and you helped keep me on track with my faith for 29 years and especially these past nine. I love you, Baby. I love your faith. I love your passion for God and for godliness. And I love being married to you.

My faith would not be worth telling about without you. There would be no "Faith" let alone anything "Great" had it not been for your love, your support, your amazingly hard work, and your encouragement. Thank you for believing in me. And thank you, my darling friend, for being the "great" in my "faith!" I love you with all my heart and this book is for you.

TABLE OF CONTENTS

FOREWORD

As the chairman of Church Growth International, I invited Pastor Wendell Smith to become a member of my board last year. His church in Seattle, Washington has applied the principles of great faith since its inception and has grown from twenty-one people to close to three thousand members. Such growth has come as Pastor Smith has exercised the principles of faith that this book discusses. He is not a man who only understands faith, he implements it through his life every day. Because of that, I would like to recommend the book by Pastor Smith entitled, *Great Faith.* This book will bring you into a greater faith in God.

In growing a church, there are five main principles that I believe are vital. First, the pastor of the church must preach the redemption of man through the Cross of Christ. I believe that truth to be important enough to preach in every sermon. Secondly, I believe the pastor should commune with the Holy Spirit continually. God is on the throne, Jesus is at His right hand–it is the Holy Spirit who lives in us. Third, I stress the importance of the pastor's personal prayer life of fellowship prayer and intercession. Fourth, I encourage every pastor to begin a small group ministry in his church. Having small groups is the natural way to do church. Finally, I believe that every pastor should have visions for his church that are beyond his own ability. Our vision is the blueprint the Holy Spirit uses to build the church upon.

Pastor Smith has exhibited these principles and his church is growing because of it. He preaches the Cross of Christ and prays continually. He has a large vision for his church and they have a ministry of small groups. I believe that his faith is great.

Hebrews 12:2 says, *"Looking unto Jesus the author and finisher of our faith; who for the joy that was set before him endured the cross, despising the shame, and is set down at the right hand of the throne of God."*

Faith is a prerequisite in doing the work of the ministry, and it is a fruit as well as a gift of the Holy Spirit. It is impossible to do the greater works of God without faith.

Pastor Smith's book on great faith will renew your hope and trust in the Lord. It will encourage you to move forward in the work of the ministry. It will inspire you to go on to greater heights with God. Greater faith is our continuous goal.

DAVID YONGGI CHO
Chairman
Church Growth International
Spring 2001

PREFACE

The Bible says that faith comes by hearing and hearing by the Word of God. You will notice that there are only a few Scripture references in the text of this book, although many Scriptures are paraphrased. For the direct quotes, references are given, but you will not find references for the paraphrased Scriptures—of which there are over five hundred. Because of that, we recommend that you search your Bible and find these references on your own. A Bible concordance can be of great help to look up and discover these wonderful verses of Scripture on your own. This will encourage you to search the Scriptures to see if these things are so, which positions you to become like the Bereans of the book of the Acts of the Apostles, who were commended for their noble spirit in doing the same.

ACKNOWLEDGEMENTS

My special thanks to many special people who have added to the success of this book in one way or another.

To our spiritual family at The City Church, The Staff, Pastors & Elders, especially to Pastor Jude & Becky Fouquier, who sacrificed everything to move to Seattle and help us pioneer our church and have led the way for a new generation in establishing Generation Church. And to Pastors Rick & Jennifer Kraker who also followed us to Seattle and helped us plant our church in 1992. Pastors Jerry & Tami, Jere, Jese and Jake McKinney also helped us lay the foundation of a new church, served us faithfully for five years and then became our first-fruits church plant to California in 1997.

And to rest of the Dream team- Pastors Don & Marlene Ostrom, Pastors Steve & Taffy Carpenter, Pastor Barbara Wright, Pastors Aaron & Cheryl Haskins, Pastors Leon & Donna Sandberg, Pastors Fred & Pam Kropp, Pastors Ed & Carol Decker and the rest of the young, up and coming Pastors and leaders of our church.

To Allen & Denise Stinnette and all our dedicated Care Pastors and teams of leaders.

To all the Generation Church cadre leaders and Generation Interns. To the dedicated City Kids staff and parents. And to the wonderful team of leaders with our Single Adult Ministry and the Young Marrieds teachers and leaders.

To the all star team who leads The City Ministries in touching our community and region.

To Kent Kessler, Jaime Jamgochian and the outstanding worship team members and singers. And to my nephew Jay & Dawn Smith, who also helped us start the church with anointed worship.

Huge thanks to our personal assistants and administrators Miss Glenda Renes and Mrs. Pam Brown.

To all our Intercessors, Pete & Joie Nordstrom, Al & Betty Porter, Eston & Patricia Catlett, Sue Jewett, Frank & Mary Erwin, Liz Oden, Sherry Dockstader, Jerry & Terry Kepler, Jacqueline Stewart, Boyd & Connie Adams, Cecille Russell and many others who have spent years praying for us.

———

To Jen Kropp-Benthin for coordinating our graphics design, and television ministry.

———

To the world's greatest Ushers, especially Rick Brown, Cliff Gerou and Jerry McNeilly, our Head Ushers. To George & Norma Jean Reece, Jon & Laura Wood, David & Erika Catlett, Scott & Tina Hay, Mark & Linda Carpenter, Dan & Dee Humphreys, Pat & Melody Jones, Rand & Maryann Galt. To Peter & Karen Henley for praying for us to come to Seattle for three and half years before we arrived.

———

To our first City churches that were sent out to San Diego, CA.- Pastors Jerry & Tami McKinney; to Arroyo Grande, CA. Pastors Rocky & Jean Tannehill. To our International churches - in Tokyo, Pastors Steven and Shelly Kaylor; and in Mexico, Pastors Phil & Judy Jaquith, and in the Philippines, Pastors Gus & Flora Tito.

———

To our personal friends, Craig & Marilyn Smith, Mike & Marsha Herron, Ken & Glenda Malmin, Wayman & Sandy Steele, Bill & Joanne Scheidler, Howard & Donna Rachinski, Rick & Merilee Johnston, Dr. Mark & Susan Jones and the late Howdy Sligar.

———

My heartfelt thanks to Dr. Kevin Conner, who imparted truth to my generation as well as others, and laid such a solid foundation of revelation and understanding in the Word of God and sound doctrine.

———

Pastor Frank & Sharon Damazio, our friends in ministry and Pastors of the great City Bible Church in Portland and true apostles to the Body of Christ.

———

Rev. Jack & Libby Louman, one of our first elders also who stood with us in faith and believed in the dream that was in us.

Rev. David Schoch, who laid many prophetic pillars into the foundation of our church and is such a dear friend.

———

My friends, Dr. Che & Sue Ahn, of Pasadena, California who helped bring spiritual refreshing to our church.

———

The Pastors of Seattle and the Eastside, especially Dr. Joe Fuiten, Pastor Tony Morris, Pastor Casey Treat, Pastor Norm Willis, Pastor Jan Hettinga, and Pastor Rick Kingham.

———

To my MFI pastor friends, the Apostolic Team, and my regional team of Pastors – Marc & Cheryl Cargill, Scott & Lori Schang, Ralph & Jacque Simmons, Doug & Lois Cotton.

———

To Larry & Yvonne Booth of Pendleton, Oregon who invested in the early months of our fledgling church.

———

Pastor Steve & Kay Valentine of Missoula, Montana who are some of my favorite people.

———

Pastors Paul & Shoddy Chase, New Life Church, Manila, Philippines.

———

To Bishop Joseph Garlington for his faith-filled support and prophetic encouragement of our congregation.

———

Dr. George & Rita Evans for their amazing prophetic direction and input into the foundations of our church.

———

Other prophetic ministries who have influenced our lives, Earnest Gentile, Mel Davis, Leonard & Rozella Fox, and Earl Bradley.

———

Our friends Pastors Bart & Coralee Pierce of City Rock Church, Baltimore, MD.

———

Dr. Don Argue, President of Northwest College in Kirkland, who encouraged me to write this book and opened a door for us in Church Growth.

Dr. Oral Roberts for coming to our church and imparting his anointing and for leading the way of faith into this new century.

Dr. Kenneth Hagin for holding two weeks of a Faith Crusade at our church in Seattle and depositing such a rich heritage of faith and healing.

Dr. Increase - Bob Harrison, who encouraged us to cast our net on the other side!

Pastor Claudio Friedzon of Buenos Aires, Argentina.

Dr. Charles Green of New Orleans, Louisiana.

Bob Weiner, my friend and apostle to nations.

John & Carol Arnott who have demonstrated for all of us the Father's heart for the church.

Dr. Marilyn Hickey for the blessing she has been to our people and for inspiring us in faith, the Word, healing, blessing and missions.

Dr. Ed Cole for modeling manhood and wisdom to our congregation.

And to Dr. David Yonngi Cho who has set such a grand standard for the 21st Century church in vision and strategic thinking, and to the outstanding staff and Board of Church Growth International.

And thanks for my holiness heritage of faith from the wonderful Church of the Nazarene and to My Northwest Nazarene University college religion professors during the years of 1968-1972, Dr. Sanner, Dr. Morris Weigelt and others.

And to Robert Jameson and Mark Daniels, and the staff of City Bible Publishing, for believing in this message.

Cast Your Net on the Other Side

Oh, magnify the LORD with me, and let us exalt His name together.
Psalm 34:3

I was awakened on that memorable Tuesday morning by an unmistakable voice. It was the closest thing to the audible voice of God I had ever experienced. It was so clear it startled me. "Cast your net on the other side!" I knew it was the Lord, and I waited for the next sentence—but nothing came. Why does God speak in phrases and make us seek for the meaning? Why does He often start a thought and then almost tease us to fill in the blank? Why does God often give only pieces, without showing us the whole puzzle? This is the walk of faith.

I pondered it all in light of having just started our new church in Seattle. It was late in the summer of 1992, and after just three weeks our fledgling church was already outgrowing the rented space at a local hotel conference room. We would soon need to move and find a bigger location.

On that morning I was a bit confused by this sudden revelation from the Lord. Had we started the church on the wrong side of town? Was I missing something? Had I missed the target of God's will? I asked all these questions but got no response. I remember praying, "Lord, if I have missed it, show me. What do you mean, 'cast your net on the other side?'"

1

On Thursday of that same week we had a church-staff meeting. Our staff consisted of myself, my office was in the den; my wife, her office was in the kitchen; and our youth pastor, Jude Fouquier, whose office was in our garage. Our staff meetings were located in the family room of our new house.

As we met for prayer and some discussion on that morning, Jude shared a word he received from the Holy Spirit. Being a one-of-a-kind prophetic-type personality, Jude has always been sensitive to the Lord's voice and consistently had the word of the Lord for us at key moments in our history. This was the beginning of many such revelations. He said the Lord had quickened a Scripture to him about "casting our net on the other side." My shocked, immediate response was, "When did you get that word?" He said he had just received it that morning. I continued probing, "What do you think it means?" Jude quickly replied, "I think it means we just do whatever He tells us to do!" I sheepishly responded, "That's what I thought too," as I smiled and acted like I had known that all along. I then told him how the Lord had spoken the same thing to me on Tuesday morning. Thank God for the prophetic advantage.

Later that same week I was invited by Pastor Casey Treat (whose great church is across town from us in Seattle) to attend a special seminar he was hosting with Bob Harrison. Having accepted the invitation, I found myself sitting in the front row that following Sunday night at Christian Faith Center. As Bob was speaking, he was pacing back and forth in front of us (he never stands still). In the middle of his message he paused at the end of my row and rested his hand on my shoulder. As he looked out at the people, he said, "I don't always know why I say the things I do, but I know when the Holy Spirit is speaking to me. He is telling some of us here tonight to 'cast our net on the other side of the boat.'" For the third time in five days I heard the word of the Lord in exactly the same vocabulary from three different sources. I sat in my chair the rest of that service pondering what the Lord was trying to tell us.

FAITH IS THE SUBSTANCE OF THINGS HOPED FOR

Hope is a wonderful thing; it is vision for the future and expectation of good for our lives. But some of us never move from hope to faith. Faith alone creates substance out of our hopes and dreams. Although we wanted and hoped for a great church, the situations that surrounded its founding demanded that we exercise great faith in fulfilling those dreams. Our prayers, worship, and seeking of God intensified as we began to exercise the principles of faith that would guide us through the process of building a church and impacting people's lives.

In doing so, we discovered that God Himself had to become our spiritual focal point. Our faith must be focused on Him alone. In order to accomplish the things He was asking of us, we needed to enlarge our faith by making Him bigger in our eyes. We sometimes limit God and think of Him as incapable of handling certain circumstances. One brother orated, "Quit speaking to God and telling Him how big your mountain is, and start speaking to your mountain and telling it how big your God is!" We are the ones that must change, not God, and our faith will therefore be increased. We have to begin to see Him for who He is and what He can do. With us, many things are impossible; but with Him nothing is impossible. There is nothing too hard for the Lord. The most astonishing discovery we made about faith was that by simply focusing on His nature and attributes instead of our problems and obstacles, the bigger God became in our eyes, the smaller our predicaments were, and the quicker we found fulfillment in His purposes.

SLEEPLESS AND SEATTLE

The process of pioneering our church started about eight months prior to receiving that amazing word from God. We had just finished the construction and dedication of two large buildings at Bible Temple in Portland, Oregon, that helped my pastor, Dick Iverson fulfill a life-long vision and celebrate forty years of ministry. A week or so after the buildings were dedicated and the ceremonies were over, I found myself agitated and irritable.

Every night for weeks I would get up in the middle of the night, unable to sleep. I would walk, pray, kneel, sing, read, and pray in the Spirit in search of relief. The most difficult thing was that I was not hearing anything from the Lord in spite of my deep desire to do so. My wife, Gini, and I had been invited to a youth conference in Cape Cod,

3

Massachusetts. One afternoon before the conference, that same spirit of agitation was on me. My wife left our hotel room with the words, "I'm going shopping. You're grouchy and you need to pray." She told me to seek God, find out what He wanted us to do, and do it. I did not like it, but I knew my wife was right. I half-heartedly thanked her for the encouragement, fell on my knees in front of that hard bed in some inexpensive hotel on the East Coast of America, and cried out to God. "Lord, I need to hear from you. Please speak to me. I'll do anything you want me to do and go anywhere you want me to go."

I had just been given a brand new Bible. It was unmarked, crisp and clean, waiting to be read. I laid it open before me and prayerfully began to read from the gospel of Matthew. Something happened when I read chapter thirteen. It had been about four weeks, over twenty-five days of sleeplessness and turmoil, but this day would change our lives forever. Kneeling in the hotel room that afternoon, heaven opened and God began to speak from the pages of the Scripture. *"The kingdom of heaven is like treasure hidden in a field, which a man found and hid; and for joy over it he goes and sells all that he has and buys that field."*[1] It went on to say, *"the kingdom of heaven is like a merchant seeking beautiful pearls, who, when he found one pearl of great price, went and sold all that he had and bought it."*[2]

Suddenly the Word of God came alive and verse after verse jumped off the pages of that new Bible as if God were speaking to me personally. He gave me a vision that day of the church we were going to have. The printed Word became the spoken Word through the work of the Holy Spirit. The Bible says, *"Faith comes by hearing, and hearing by the word of God."*[3] Faith was ignited in my heart that day. The faith that comes by hearing a Word from God was breathing life into my spirit. The *rhema*–Word of God was speaking directly to me. I highlighted all those verses with a fluorescent yellow marker. By the time that week was over, I must have marked several hundred verses. From that time of wrestling with God came confirmation of the location of our church, the timing for planting, and even the name of our congregation. That particular Bible became a special treasure to me and still, to this day, is marked and anointed of God as the instrument God used to speak life and direction into my soul.

IT IS NOT YOUR CHURCH

Several months later, my wife and I made a special trek to the Oregon coast. It was the spring of 1992 and about six months before we planned to launch our church. We took three days to seek God, pray, walk the beautiful beaches near Haystack Rock, and journal our thoughts. We determined to write down everything we wanted in a church, believing that the Lord would help us frame and build that kind of congregation. Having traveled extensively across America for the previous five years, we had a good idea of the things we did and did not want in our church. We wrote down everything that our hearts desired but soon learned it was not that easy.

From those three days of meditation and brainstorming came the Twelve Covenants of The City Church that expresses our core values as a congregation. We also had many other ideas and thoughts of what we hoped to do one day. Some of those things we have accomplished but most have been placed on the Holy Ghost shelf of waiting on the Lord. God gives creativity and talent as gifts to us, but they can sometimes get in the way of faith because we lean on our abilities instead of trusting God for direction and daily guidance. If we could do it ourselves, we would not need faith in God to achieve it and could therefore subtly become independent of the One we are serving.

We discovered within the first few weeks of church planting that we could not just initiate something because it was a good idea. We actually had to pray, wait on God, and get His permission before we could implement a plan. The Holy Spirit became the functional leader of our church. We were responsible to listen to His prompting and walk in obedience. Our responsibility was to faithfully seek Him and diligently wait upon Him until we heard His voice clearly.

Obedience is more than just obeying the general commands of Scripture. Obedience to His voice is also required of a mature leader. The Holy Spirit still speaks to believers today and delights to lead us into the perfect will of God. But we must be patient and sensitive to hear His voice. *"For as many as are led by the Spirit of God, these are the sons of God."*[4] Jesus is the Good Shepherd who speaks to His sheep and *"they know His voice."*[5]

In the New Testament era, God spoke to His people in a variety of ways. Of course, He spoke to us through His son, Jesus while He was on earth and through His anointed words that were recorded. But after Jesus was raised from the dead and had ascended, He poured out His Spirit on the first generation Church and led them into the fulfillment of His commission. The apostles and early church disciples knew the glory of being led by God, and they subsequently made wise, Holy Spirit-led decisions that affected the entire Church of those days. They had the inner witness of the Holy Spirit. They received revelation and insight from the Holy Spirit through prophecies and speaking in tongues. The Lord appeared to them in visions and trances. Angels appeared to many and gave them divine assistance. Eventually, the apostles traveled the world and wrote letters to the churches they planted, giving them what we now know and love as the New Testament Scriptures. Thank God for those wonderful revelations from God of His ways and His truth.

God still leads His Church today and will use many supernatural means to confirm to us what He wants to do in our lives. Just because the canon of Scripture has been finished does not mean that God no longer desires to speak and guide us in His ways and will. The revelations of today are, of course, not on the level of Scripture; but the Lord will use those thoughts, dreams, visions, and that inner voice of the Holy Spirit to lead and encourage us. The inspired Scriptures are then the rule, standard, and means by which all such revelations are judged.

My first lesson in faith was to recognize that it was not my church–it was His. He was speaking clearly to me to obey Him and cast my ministry nets exactly where He said, not necessarily where I wanted. I had to acknowledge that Jesus was the Chief Shepherd and I was His associate. It came as a true revelation to me that I could not do whatever I wanted. It was not our church. It was His church, and I was a man under command. As we pioneered our church in the autumn of that inaugural year, we started on a journey of faith that became an ongoing discovery of how God works and what faith really means. It did not take long to realize that the Lord wanted to be the One in charge and that He fully expected me to obey Him in all respects, seek Him diligently in prayer, and discover on a daily basis His unfolding plan for our growing congregation.

OUR FIRST TEST OF FAITH

Once we moved to Seattle, the first great challenge of faith for us was to find a place to settle as a congregation. Twenty-one people committed to help start the church and moved with us from Portland to Seattle. Forty-two were in attendance at the first meeting we held. Meeting at the Bellevue Marriott Hotel, our services were soon running about seventy-five. Within three weeks we outgrew the space and the hotel was asking us to leave. Thus began the great adventure of looking for that special location where our little church could let down its roots. I recall the sense of desperation we felt as we wondered how we were going to find a place suitable for us within one week. When faced with a seemingly impossible situation, a practical faith is needed. Faith seems even more accessible when our backs are up against a wall and the situation demands it.

A real estate broker showed us several buildings, most of which needed remodeling and a lot of creative thinking for use as a church. After hours of looking at a variety of sites, he recalled a place that had just become available for lease and according to his estimation, might be ideal for us. The space was a second-story office area in a retail strip of stores adjacent to a K-Mart, located at 148th and Main Street in Bellevue. There was eleven thousand square feet of space, but it was badly in need of work and had been vacant for almost two years.

When Jude and I walked in, we knew it was the place for us. We had told our little congregation that we would telephone and let them know where we would be meeting the next Sunday. The Lord had spoken to my heart that week from a Scripture in Isaiah, that He would *"make the crooked places straight."*[6] I believed that we would move straight to the next location and would have confirmation that this was the direction of the Lord. This new building was located straight down 148th Avenue, south of the hotel. It was easy to find, accessible for everyone, and a very visible location to start a new church. We asked the landlord if we could show it to our people. Amazingly, he gave us the key and said we could meet there on Sunday and even occupy it for a few weeks to see if it met our needs. We could hardly believe it. We called everyone with the new directions to our potential church home.

IN THE MOUTH OF TWO OR THREE WITNESSES

The most remarkable thing happened that same day. At the same time we were finding the new space, some materials arrived in the mail. Five months earlier I had sent away for a demographic study of Bellevue, Washington. In order to provide statistics, the company asked us to designate an intersection in the area. They then supply the information based on concentric circles from that focal point. We were astonished to find that I had chosen that same intersection five months before. The header on every page of those demographic studies included the name of our church and the address. It read, "The City Church, 148th & Main, Bellevue, Washington." We were negotiating a lease at the exact location God had directed me to choose for the demographic study before we even moved to town. I had randomly chosen it off a city map, but obviously the Lord was guiding me!

On that same day, we were speaking with the landlord about the ethnic diversity of people we noticed walking through the shops and down the sidewalks. Our mission statement, which we believed was motivated by the Holy Spirit, was to minister to "young and old, rich and poor, red and yellow, black and white." As we chatted, the landlord interjected, "Oh yeah, the city calls this neighborhood the little United Nations." We found ourselves in the center of the most diverse community on the Eastside of Seattle.

Sometime later that same historic day, I remembered a prophecy by Prophet David Schoch that he had given us three months before we were sent out from our church in Portland. I recalled him sharing something that related to the location for our new church. I found the tape and listened for the part where he suddenly stopped his message, looked down at my wife and me in the front row, and from the pulpit prophesied this incredible word: "I believe there is a place where you are going that is going to be the crossroads of two main boulevards. And when you get there, it will be a great joy to know the Lord prepared it for you beforehand." He spoke of a crossroads. The community where this space was located was called the "Crossroads" community. Then he mentioned streets and used the terms "main" and "boulevard." I looked up the word "boulevard" in my Webster's dictionary and found this definition: "A wide, often landscaped thoroughfare." Main Street and a four-lane boulevard bordered the intersection of our new location. 148th Avenue in Bellevue is a beautifully landscaped four-lane street, a primary arterial through that part of the city.

To our great amazement almost one hundred people showed up for church that Sunday. I shared with them some of these signs from the Lord. We had a breathtaking sense of His presence, favor, and sovereign direction. That sense has never left our church. To this day, we get emotional thinking of God's mighty hand working on our behalf. I am confident that being obedient to His leading in "casting our net on the other side" was the key to God honoring our faith.

ARE YOU A FAITH CHURCH?

People often ask me if I am a faith preacher and if our church is a faith church. My response is always the same. What other kind of preacher or church is there? I certainly would not want to be an unbelief preacher, and I would not want our church to be a place of skepticism and tradition, void of genuine faith in a powerful God. But when some people think of faith, they think of a particular church or a movement. We need to think of God instead. Faith was His idea and the result of hearing a word from Him! Faith is a Bible concept, and everyone who is called by His name should embrace it.

I was reared in the holiness denomination of the Church of the Nazarene, in which my father was a pastor for many years. I am very proud of that heritage. I was later tutored under the balanced ministry of Pastor Dick Iverson, serving for twenty years on his staff at Bible Temple (now City Bible Church) in Portland, Oregon. His roots and heritage came out of a relationship with Evangelist T.L. Osborne. We were consequently influenced by a revival atmosphere that was sprinkled with holiness and solid teaching on the glorious and prophetic Church of the last days. However, I had very little direct exposure to the faith message and movement until the last few years of the 20th century.

Although I would not categorize myself as a formal part of the faith movement, I have been blessed to know many of the great men and women of that stream and have always been strengthened by their emphasis on faith. My revelation of faith did not originate from the teaching or training of men, it came by the instruction of the Holy

9

Spirit through desperation and need for God. When we pioneered The City Church on the eastside of Seattle in 1992, we needed faith. We were attempting to plant a church in one of the Northwest's most expensive cities. We found ourselves in the high rent district but discovered that when we are in God's will, it is God's bill. His vision will bring His provision. Faith was the only constant we were holding onto and as our history unfolded, we had no idea how much we would need it. We would need faith for finances, faith for harvest, faith for wisdom, faith for strategy, and faith for miracles. We had to be obedient to God's word to us and cast our net on the other side.

CAST

We have to cast the net. The net is not designed to be showcased on the wall of a fishing museum. Instead, we need to cast that thing. Let it fly. Get it out of the boat and into the water. An old fishing buddy, notorious for quoting fishing proverbs, once reminded me, "He who does not put line in water does not catch fish." The net was made for casting, for fishing, for snagging the big ones. The fishermen of Jesus' day crafted, cleaned, and mended their nets for the purpose of fishing. We must decide today what action God is requiring of us and then step out. Walk in obedience. Do what He tells us. Obey His commands. Launch out into the deep. Cast that net.

YOUR NET

A net must be carefully constructed or crafted to be useful. There must be a plan, scenario, and strategy. It has to be woven together to be ready for the catch. This is not some halfhearted bundle of strings. This is an earnest, well thought out, labor intensive net. It is fabricated from strong materials—people who know fishing designed it. It is crafted to meet the demands of fishing and the topography of the lake. It is made to endure, to be used over and over in the occupation of fishing. This was the trade and livelihood of Peter, James, and John. Their subsistence depended upon this net. Our life and faith depend on ours. We need to build it, get it ready, and allow God to bless it and fill it with fish.

We need to cast our net—use what we have. God will give us our own revelation, direction, and plan. We cannot borrow someone else's net and have success. To compare our net with another's will only bring frustration. God did not give us another person's net, he gave us our own personal nets. We need to wash it, mend it, and do all we can to ready it for use. God intends to bless our nets and to work within the framework of our calling and gifting. He designed us with our personalities and deposited within us the gifts of grace. That unique combination of style, mannerisms, and divinely-ordained anointing will be a powerful force to accomplish what God has destined for us.

THE OTHER SIDE

Miracles are on the other side. That is where David slew Goliath. That is where Jonathan and his armor bearer took on the garrison of the Philistines and broke the tyranny of their enemy. The other side is where Jesus sent His disciples, knowing that a legion of demons awaited them on the shore and a storm would hinder them as they traveled. That was where the miracle awaited them, on the other side. The other side was where he told them to cast their nets and catch that miraculous load of fish.

When Jesus told Peter to cast his net on the other side of the boat, it was not the different side of the boat that produced the miracle. It was a matter of obedience. It was doing what He said. It was dependence upon the Master. It was trusting in God. It was faith!

A seasoned preacher, well into his seventies, once commented to some up-and-coming young pastors, "If I was forty again, I would attempt something so awesome for God that He would be embarrassed not to bring it to pass." That statement stirred me to plant a church in my forties and run boldly in the will of God.

When was the last time we attempted something big for God? If we want to see God begin to move in our lives in unprecedented fashion, we need to cast our nets on the other side. Launch out into the deep parts. Take that new step of faith. Risk something. Do something for the first time. Be bold in our faith. God loves it. We need to go over to the other side and see what miracles await us.

HE IS LORD

He is the Lord of the wind and the sea. Even they obey Him. He tells us to cast our nets on the other side and provides a miraculous, net-breaking, catch of fish. He will do the same with men. If we are willing and obedient, we will eat the good of the land. He will enable us to do *"exceedingly abundantly above all that we could ask or think, according to the power that works in us."*[7]

The Lord my God is with me wherever I go. He will never leave me or forsake me. Every place the sole of my foot treads upon He has given me. Whatever I put my hand to will be blessed. If I meditate on His Word day and night, I will be like a tree planted by the rivers of water. My leaf will not wither and I will bear fruit in my season, whatever I do will prosper. If I meditate in His law, I will make my way prosperous and I will surely have good success. He said He would never leave me or forsake me and be with me wherever I go.

CHAPTER TWO

Making God Big

I will praise the name of God with a song,
and will magnify Him with thanksgiving.
Psalm 69:30

I do not remember exactly when we first said it, but I remember the response. I was making a transition in one of our services, and the people were excited. We had been singing celebration songs and the anointing was present, bringing hope, grace, and strength. I said to our congregation, "We believe in a great big God and a little bitty devil." They loved and believed it because that statement expressed our philosophy of worship and faith in God. Unfortunately, too many believers have a small God and a huge devil; that kind of theology will hurt us. What we think of God is central to our faith. According to the Scriptures, the Devil is small enough to fit under our feet and God is big enough to fill both heaven and earth. Our God is huge! He is mighty! He is everywhere and knows everything! He is worthy of all our praise, honor, and worship.

As a pastor, I often take a peek at our people during the worship portion of our service. I have rarely seen them looking back at me—they are usually lost in God, deep into their communion with Him. Our church was born in strong worship and praise. We have never had a problem worshiping God. Thanksgiving, adoration, and exaltation of the Lord abound where God's people truly love Him because as Christians, that is our great joy. This is how we make God big—we worship Him and think of Him as He is, bigger than anything in the Universe.

ANSWER MAN

When my children were very young, we used to play a game called "Answer Man" before putting them to bed at night. They could ask any question they wanted and I would give them the answer. I was the "Answer Man" and, at their age, I had the answers. If I did not know the answer, I acted like I did and they did not know the difference. One night our son Judah, about age three, asked his toughest question, "Daddy, where...where...where did God come from?" With his brain working faster than his mouth, he stuttered a little. I said, "He didn't come from anywhere, buddy, He is God and He has always been there." He was not satisfied, "No, Daddy, I mean who...who...who was His parents?" I replied, "He doesn't have parents son, He is God." He plowed on, "No...no, I mean who...who...who was His mommy and His daddy?" "Judah, God doesn't have a mommy and a daddy. He was not born. He has just always been there. He is God." With glimpses of his future theological inquisitiveness he kept going, "No...no, Daddy, who...who...where did He...how...how...?" By now it was late and bedtime had already passed, so I finally interrupted and said, "Son, I don't know. Nobody knows. And you'll never know. So let's just go to sleep."

We cannot explain God. We cannot contain God. We cannot understand God. We have to simply believe God and appreciate His magnitude. This is the God who has planned all things, including the details of our lives. This is the God who has saved us and forgiven us of our sins. This is the God who did the signs and miracles of the Old and New Testaments. He is the same yesterday, today, and forever and He is working in our lives to do mighty things. He is unfathomable and incomparable. He is the Matchless One. He is the Mighty One of Israel. He is the Maker of heaven and earth. He is the God who can rescue us out of every problem, help us in any difficulty, and empower us for any situation. Look at Him. He is amazing. His power is limitless. His understanding is unfathomable. His grace is incomprehensible. He is God. There is no other like Him. This is the God we are called upon to believe in, trust, and follow. This is the God that not only expects faith but will actually inspire the faith we need to trust Him.

If we keep our eyes on Him, faith will grow in our hearts. If we focus on our enemies or our problems, unbelief will dominate. If we expect to go to new levels of faith, we may need a new vision of God. In that case, we need to read our Bible, speak it out loud, attend more church services, listen to more tapes, and read more edifying books. Doing so will allow us to build our faith and see our God for who He really is. He is the unconquered Conqueror. He is our Helper. He is our Lord and Master. He is the all-encompassing One, the God who is everything we need Him to be.

One of the fond memories of our son's childhood occurred when he was about age four, after we put him in the bathtub one night. I started the bath water, placed him in it, gave him his little rubber toys, and walked out of the room to get something. Within a minute we heard a shriek from the bathroom. "Daddy. Mommy, it's overflowing, it's overflowing!" My wife and I simultaneously rushed toward the bathroom from different parts of the house, fully expecting to see water cascading over the side of the tub, onto the bathroom floor, and into our basement. We frantically arrived to find the water level in the tub far from overflowing. A little frustrated, I corrected Judah for the outburst. With a cute little sheepish grin on his face, he looked up at us and innocently said, "Daddy what's overflowing mean?"

Some of us are like that with our problems. We are feeling overwhelmed, while our wonderful heavenly Father is quite in control of the matter. We think we are going to drown in our difficulties, but God already has His hand in our rescue. Peter thought he was going to sink to the bottom of the lake, but Jesus said, *"Why did you doubt?"*[1] and reached out and took hold of him to put him back into the safety of the boat. As with Peter, there will be times when His hand will be extended to us to get us out of a problem. We cannot let fear or weakness hold us back from stepping out to walk on water. God can handle our weakness. Our obedience is what He is looking for. Water walking is worth the risk of sinking. In the midst of our problems, we need to go ahead and get our feet wet. If He was the One who said, "Come," then we should exercise our faith through obedience, get out of our boat, and walk!

The first purpose of a church is to glorify God. We are the collective franchise outlets of His glorious kingdom. We are the local spiritual retailers where people can shop for God's goods. We are the art museum where they can see His miraculous works. We are the divine deli where folks can taste and see that the Lord is good. Our task is to magnify Him, to make Him big. Our responsibility is to lift Him up in such a way that He is attractive to others. Our role is to get God up where He belongs, so that when people see Him, they will marvel at His greatness and be drawn to His nature. King David wrote in the Psalms, *"Oh, magnify the LORD with me, and let us exalt His name together!"*[2] In reality, David knew (and we realize) that we cannot make God any bigger. There is nothing finite man can do to change the infinite One. We can only make Him bigger in our own understanding, bigger in our own eyes. The Hebrew word translated "magnify" means, "to cause to grow, to make great or powerful." The Psalms uses other words, like "exalt—to lift up and set on high" or "extol—to esteem highly and prize." In our own perception, God is enlarged and gets bigger. We begin to fathom His greatness and His attributes, and our faith grows similarly.

MULTIPLIED ANOINTING

When a group of believers come together there is a multiplied anointing. The impact of a corporate gathering is amplified many times more than that of a personal encounter with God. Our personal prayer closet cannot compare with the family room of God's gatherings. Our private moments with Him are not in the same class as a visitation of God with His beloved Church. This is where miracles happen. One hundred and twenty people were forever inaugurated into church history when the Holy Spirit was poured out on their humble meeting in the now-famous Upper Room. Peter and John gave the lame man more than silver and gold at the gate of a gathering. Little Rhoda had the surprise of her life when the imprisoned apostle Peter showed up at the door of the all-church prayer meeting.

The anointing can destroy any yoke of the Devil. The anointing of one believer is strong. The anointing of two believers is multiplied ten times. Imagine the combined anointed power available to a gathering of believers who are all exercising faith and are in the sweet agreement of biblical unity. Under the influence of that kind of anointing, a believer can receive an answer from God in an instant. One moment in His presence can change our lives forever. One short time under that influence of grace can answer questions, solve riddles, open the heavens, and heal the body. Nothing is impossible in an atmosphere of faith. The Bible says, *"the yoke will be destroyed because of the anointing."*[3] Power-packed anointing is released through faith, especially the combined faith of a large group of confident believers.

Our problems that seem so overwhelming can be made small in the light of His greatness. That trouble that was making us miserable on Monday, testing us on Tuesday, winding us up on Wednesday, thrashing us on Thursday, frustrating us on Friday, and slaying us on Saturday becomes subjected on Sunday. In light of His greatness, our difficulties become petty, trifling, minute, trivial, paltry, insignificant, and microscopic. He is bigger than our problems. He is bigger than any opposition. He is bigger than any disease. He is bigger than any question we have. He is bigger than our frustration. He is bigger than our struggle. He is bigger than our crisis.

Twelve spies were sent in by Moses to spy out the Promised Land. Ten of them came back with their eyes on the giants, the cities, the walls, and the enemy. Only two, Joshua and Caleb, had a different spirit of faith. They wholly followed the Lord. They believed in the power and might of their God. The ten evil men who were filled with unbelief died in the wilderness along with the generation of unbelievers they led. God swore that they would not enter the Promised Land. Hebrews says they could not enter in because of unbelief.

During the week there can be a shrinking of our faith. That is why we need to attend church every Sunday and let the Holy Spirit and the Word of faith work in us. In worship, where God is magnified among His people and we are transformed into His image from glory to glory, we see Him as He is—big! The anointing is multiplied. We get over our Monday murmurings, our Tuesday trials, and our Saturday sufferings. We are transformed into His image. God is exalted up above our tribulations. We come into His presence on Sunday and He lifts us up. He is the lifter up of our heads. He is magnified in our eyes. After worship, our hearts are a tilled field that is ready to receive the seed of the eternal Word of God. It is then that we begin to believe that our God can do anything.

WHEN GOD IS MADE BIG

When we first started our church it was evident that His presence in the ministry of worship was very important. We recognized His power and came to appreciate the unusually strong anointing on our meetings. Our Sunday gatherings became manifestations of His glory. We witnessed lives being dramatically changed in a single service. Marriages were restored. Bodies were healed. Minds were set free. Needs were met. Problems were solved, and enemies were defeated.

We have a strong confidence that if people will come into the Lord's presence, they will be touched, blessed, and helped by His power. We believe there is extraordinary hope and help in His presence, a holy assistance that only He can produce. It is not the quality of our music or the wisdom of our oratory that will bring that kind of divine intervention. It is not the skill of our special songs or the depth of talent in our choir. It is simply our worship and exaltation of God that will create an atmosphere of faith where miracles happen. The primary purpose of our church service is to exalt Him, magnify Him, and make Him big in the eyes of the people so that their faith can rest in the power of God, not in the wisdom of men.

When God is made big, problems are made small. When God is made big, demons tremble, cower, and flee. When God is made big, diseases shrivel. When God is made big, mountains are moved into the sea. When God is made big, darkness is dispelled by light. When God is made big, answers to questions come easily. When God is made big, confusion lifts and direction comes. When God is made big, idols topple. When God is made big, unbelief gives way to great faith, the weakest Christian becomes mighty, and even fools cannot err in the ways of God. When God is made big, the narrow way becomes a boulevard and the desert a spring of water. The widow is covered and the orphan is sheltered when God is made big. When He is made big, the aged are strengthened and the young are protected; there are no enemies that can intimidate and no devils that can operate. When God is made big, believers rejoice and shout for victory and the frailest among us becomes a mighty overcomer! When God is made big, death loses its sting and the *"valley of the shadow"*[4] becomes a passage of promotion. *"Oh, magnify the LORD with me, and let us exalt His name together!"*[5]

It does not take much to magnify Him. Just read His Word. Read it out loud. Read it until it begins to take hold in our hearts. Read it until it is personal. Read it until it reverberates in our spirits and dominates our minds. Read the Psalms. Read the Proverbs. Read of the battles He has won. Read of His mighty acts and His valiant deeds. Read of those who believed Him and how they overcame. Meditate on the power of our God.

The reason an entire book of the Old Testament is named for remembrance is because God knew His people's tendency to forget. Moses warned the people in the book of Deuteronomy to *"beware, lest you forget"*[6] the Lord your God. One generation would pass and the next would forget His awesome deeds. One generation might experience His power, but the next could be ignorant of it if the Word is not freshly encountered.

Every generation is admonished to pass the truth and passion for God to the next. How easily we forget what the Lord did for us. We forget how He saved us and delivered us from a dead-end road. We forget how He set us free from an addiction. We forget His healing touch that released our body from pain. We forget His loving mercy and how He overlooked our stumbling and transgressions. We forget how He helped us in a crisis or the vow we uttered to Him in secret. It does not take long to fall back into old habits of thought and forget the goodness of God.

Let us change our ways and focus on His greatness and His goodness. Let us muse on His awesome power and His majesty. Mutter His powerful deeds through the pages of the biblical record. Repeat His great names and titles. Remind ourselves who we are serving—the God of the whole earth!

THE NAMES AND TITLES OF GOD

God is revealed in the Old Testament as the *"commander of the Lord's armies,"*[7] the *"defender of widows,"* the *"father of the fatherless."*[8] *"He is called the God of the whole earth,"*[9] *"the God who does wonders,"*[10] and the God *"who forgives."*[11]

Elohim, the Hebrew word for God, reveals him as *El Elohe* Israel—God the God of Israel; *El Elyon*—the Most High God; *El Olam*—the Everlasting God; *El Roi*—the One Who Sees; and *El Shaddai*—God Almighty.

His name is *YAH, Yahweh* or *Jehovah*, the Lord who is Salvation. He is *Jehovah Gmolah*—the God of Recompense; *Jehovah Jireh*—the Lord Who Will Provide and *Jehovah Maccaddeshem*—the Lord My Sanctifier. He is *Jehovah Makkeh*—the Lord Who Strikes; *Jehovah Nissi*—the Lord Our Banner and *Jehovah Rapha*—the Lord Our Healer. He is also *Jehovah Rohi*—the Lord My Shepherd; *Jehovah Sabbaoth*—the Lord of Hosts; *Jehovah Shalom*—the Lord Our Peace; *Jehovah Shammah*—the Lord Who is Present; and *Jehovah Tsidkenu*—the Lord Our Righteousness.

David called Him the one *"who took me out of my mother's womb,"*[12] who dwells between the cherubim, and *"who hears the prayer."*[13] The king of the Psalms also named Him, *"my exceeding joy,"*[14] my guide even to death, *"my hiding place and shield,"*[15] *"the horn of my salvation,"*[16] *"my keeper,"*[17] *"my fortress,"*[18] *"my glory and the One who lifts up my head,"*[19] *"my light and my salvation,"*[20] *"my portion forever,"*[21] *"my Redeemer,"*[22] and *"my strong refuge."*[23] He is *"the LORD mighty in battle,"*[24] *"the LORD on high,"*[25] *"the LORD our Maker,"*[26] and *"the LORD who made heaven and earth."*[27] He is a *"Rock,"*[28] a *"shade at your right hand,"*[29] the *"Shepherd of Israel,"*[30] *"a shield for me,"*[31] *"the strength of my heart,"*[32] *"my stronghold,"*[33] *"a sun and a shield,"*[34] *"a very present help in trouble."*[35] He is the Potter and we are the clay.

Jesus Christ is the *"LORD who has mercy,"*[36] *"the LORD who is faithful,"*[37] *"the LORD who makes a way in the sea,"*[38] and *"the High and Lofty One who inhabits eternity."*[39] He is the *"Alpha and the Omega, the Beginning and the End, the First and the Last,"*[40] *"He who lives and was dead,"*[41] and who has *"the keys of Hades and of Death."*[42] Jesus was revealed in the gospel of John as I AM. He Himself said, *"I am the bread of life,"*[43] *"I am the door,"*[44] *"I am the good shepherd,"*[45] *"I am the light of the world,"*[46] *"I am the resurrection and the life,"*[47] *"I am the vine,"*[48] *"I am the way, the truth and the life."*[49]

Our Lord was also given many other illustrious names and titles.

He is our holy advocate, our anointed attorney, defending us against an evil prosecutor. He is also the judge who rules righteously and declares us free. He is not only the author of our faith, but He is the finisher of it. He started a good work and He will complete it. He is the *"Beginning and the End, the First and the Last."*[50] He is the *"Apostle and High Priest of our confession."*[51] He is the great bishop of our souls, the bridegroom of our heart, the Chief Shepherd of our church, and the Cornerstone of our foundation. He is the Amen, making it so for us. We see Him glorious as the Bright and morning star, the DayStar that is arising in our hearts. He is the Forerunner who has gone inside the veil for us and secured an anchor for our souls. He is our Priest and Rabbi, Prince and Prophet, Teacher and King, Lord and Savior, Minister and Master. He is the Wonderful Counselor, the Mighty God, the Ever-lasting Father, and the Prince of Peace. He is the Lion and the Lamb. He is the only blessed Potentate, the great Son of God and Son of Man.

Jesus is given the titles of the Great Physician, the Judge, the Head of the Church, and the Friend of sinners. He is the Redeemer, Refiner, Servant, and Sacrifice. He is the Rod out of the root of Jesse, the beautiful Rose of Sharon, and the Lily of the Valley. He is Shiloh. He is the *"Stone that the builders rejected,"*[52] but He *"has become the cornerstone, a stone of stumbling and a rock of offense."*[53] He is the Door, the Guide, the Teacher, and the Master. He is our deliverer, Emmanuel, God with us. He is the only *"mediator between God and men, the man Christ Jesus."*[54] How can we not bow down and worship Him?

PSALMS FROM THE MESSAGE BIBLE

Eugene Peterson has given the Body of Christ, and generations to come, a delightful paraphrase of the Scriptures in The Message Bible. His use of language to describe God is both charming and refreshing.

From his writing of the Psalms, he calls God the "brilliant Lord, with a household name that echoes around the world." He writes, calling God "the bedrock under my feet, the castle in which I live, and my rescuing knight." He refers to God as the "Just One, the Kind One, the heaven-dwelling God." He gives God new titles, "Guardian God," "Strong King," "Lover of Justice," "the One and Only Wonder-Working God," "Sky-Rider—striding the ancient skies," "Ear-Maker," "Eye-Shaper,"

"God of the Angel Armies," "Earth-Tamer," "Ocean-Pourer," "Mountain-Maker," "Hill-Dresser," "Muzzler of sea storms," "Father of orphans," "champion of widows."

There are not words enough to describe God effectively, but with words like these we have fresh insight into who He is. He is "beautifully, gloriously robed, dressed up in sunshine," "sheer beauty, all-generous in love, loyal always and ever." He is "robed and ruling" and "surging with strength." "His terrible beauty makes the gods look cheap. All sunshine and sovereign is God, generous in gifts and glory."

How are we to praise Him? How about, "Call out 'Bravo!' to God, the High God of Israel, for God is great, and worth a thousand Hallelujahs? Applause, everyone. Bravo, bravissimo! Shout God-songs at the top of your lungs!" What a fresh way to worship the Lord God.

Peterson paraphrases Psalm 145: "Your beauty and splendor have everyone talking; Your marvelous doings are headline news; I could write a book full of the details of your greatness. The fame of your goodness spreads across the country."

Everyone has praise language within him or her. If we journal, write songs, collect great quotes, keep memorabilia, or just love to worship God, we ought to accumulate our own list of God-songs and divine lyrics, magnifying God with our own words. I asked our staff at The City Church to share with me some praise phrases they use in their worship. They submitted the following lines of love:

> "You are everything I need, God; you are my friend, my doctor, my dentist, my real estate agent, my administrative assistant, my father, my husband, my banker, my friend."
>
> "Lord, You stir my Kool-Aid. Lord, You rock my party. Lord, You dominate my life. You're the master of my universe."
>
> "God, I love who You are."
>
> "Yes, Sir, You're my Captain. You're my point man. You sweep me off my feet. You're a lavish Father."
>
> "You are all that I need and I need all that You are!"

WHO HE IS

One of my objectives as a pastor is to help others focus on the Lord instead of their problems. We all need to overcome small thinking when it comes to God. We tend to focus on the problem instead of the Maker of solutions. We focus on the created thing instead of the Creator. We focus on the temporal resistance instead of the eternal Conqueror. Magnifying God is not accomplished through preaching alone, there is also great power in praise and worship. There is power in magnifying and exalting Him. When He is lifted up He will draw all men to Himself. When we praise Him, He comes. The Bible tells us He is *"enthroned in the praises of Israel."*[55] He is enthroned on our praises. When we truly worship, we enter another world—the supernatural realm of the Spirit where the Lord resides and liberty rules. It is there that God meets us.

We have seen many people come to church still distant from the supernatural Source, walking afar off from the mighty One and blind to the power of the Rescuer. Through anointed worship in Spirit and in truth, they are drawn into His magnificent presence. It is in this place of His *Shekinah* glory, in His anointed and life-giving presence, that people are changed.

The apostle Paul had a revelation that believers are changed from glory to glory into the image of the Lord. David said it happened at the time of the evening sacrifice. Solomon saw it happen when the cloud descended on the finished Temple and the priests could no longer stand. Elijah saw it happen when the fire came down from heaven and consumed the sacrifice, the altar, the stones, and the water around it. Peter, James, and John saw it happen when their Master was transfigured in that holy place on the mountain. The early church saw it happen when the power and fire of God in the place of worship and prayer touched 120 people. We too can see His glory and lead people to that pleasant and powerful place where miracles happen. It is here that faith is the strongest and people's lives can be changed in a moment.

The Bible refers to the spirit of faith. I believe there is an atmosphere of faith created by our adoration, which escorts us into that atmosphere of the miraculous. People must be taught that they can go there daily, to the throne of grace, and find mercy to help them when in need. We need to make Him big, exalt Him, lift Him up, and watch the miraculous begin to take place around us in the lives of others.

GOD SEEKING US

What would it be like to have God seeking us? Think of it. He is seeking us to bless us, provide for us, make us successful, help us, give us special aid and favor, and to show Himself strong on our behalf. The Bible says that God is seeking true worshippers, those who worship Him *"in spirit and truth."*[56] He is seeking those who hearts are loyal and faithful and perfect toward Him. He is seeking those who will magnify Him and exalt Him and lift Him up so that others may be drawn to Him. He is looking for true worshippers. He is looking for magnifiers. He is looking for exalters. He is seeking those who will make Him big, so that people will see Him as He really is.

Several new series of automobiles have built-in computers that can track a car and tell the driver, via satellite, exactly where he is at any time. They can observe him through the global positioning system and send assistance to him in an emergency. He can be searched for and found. If we will become true worshipers, God will search us out and find us. He will track us down and bless us. He will determine our location to pinpoint His blessing on us. He will download His special favor and set us up for incredible success. Worship releases His presence and His blessing. When we bless the Lord, His blessing comes back upon us. Are we looking for a blessing on our business? We should then worship Him. Are we praying for favor on our families? Then we need to bless the Lord. Do we desire the increased blessing of God on our church? Then we should motivate the entire congregation to become lovers of God. God is looking for that kind of people, and He is seeking us out.

WHAT CAN WE GIVE THE GOD WHO HAS EVERYTHING?

Years ago I discovered a profound truth. There was nothing I could do to impress God. We are human, and He is divine. We are finite, and He is infinite. He is almighty, and we are weak. There is nothing we can do to make Him say, "Wow!" I realized I could not sound spiritual enough, pray accurately enough, exercise enough authority, or be holy enough to impress Almighty God. We cannot give enough money, do enough good deeds, or perform enough righteous acts to secure His amazement.

There is only one thing that we humans, made in the image of God, can do to bless God. Worship Him! Give Him our praise. Give Him our love. Give Him our adoration. Tell Him how great He is. Use all known adjectives in attempting to describe Him. Deplete our word bank expressing His wonder. Empty our spiritual thesaurus portraying Him. Exhaust our emotional reserves endeavoring to pay tribute to Him. Praise Him with all our heart, and let Him know we love Him with everything that is within us. Such deeds will bless Him.

Like a father whose little child crawls up on his lap to hug him and tell him how much he loves him, so our heavenly Father is blessed with our love and affection expressed toward Him. When our children, Wendy and Judah, were small, I used to regularly affirm my love by playfully declaring, "If I could line up all the little boys and little girls in the whole wide world, and choose any of them, I would choose you." They would squeal in response and hug me as tight as they could and exclaim, "Daddy, you're the best daddy in the whole wide world." Heart words like those make an impression. Most fathers would give anything to hear those kinds of words. To have children who respond to our love, appreciate us, and give us their undivided affection makes every sacrifice worthwhile. We would do anything for them. Such expressions of our love for God will fulfill what Jesus called the greatest of all the commandments—that we love the Lord our God with all our heart, soul, and mind. We will be like King David who had a heart after God's and said, *"I will bless the Lord at all times, His praise shall continually be in my mouth."*[57]

GOD IS GOOD

He is the same God yesterday, today, and forever. He hasn't changed. He has always been good. He is still good. He is still gracious, loving, and kind. He is still merciful and abounding in goodness. He still does miracles. The God who did miracles in the Old Testament and was manifest through Jesus Christ in the New Testament (and performed great signs and wonders) will do them for us. The God who anointed the apostles of the first-generation Church with the Holy Spirit and power, and did amazing wonders through them, will do wonders through us in our generation.

The God who stopped the mouths of lions in Daniel's den can stop the mouths of those who speak against us. The God who delivered Shadrach, Meshach, and Abednego out of the fiery furnace can deliver us out of our trial and temptation. The God who opened the Red Sea for Moses and caused the waters of the Jordan to stand up in a heap for Joshua can make a way for us where there seems to be no way. The God who turned the water into wine at the wedding in Cana of Galilee can turn our crisis into a miracle. The God who compelled all the animals of the earth to enter the Ark of Noah can speak to people and draw them to our churches, businesses, or to us personally to meet our needs. The God who filled the Temple of Solomon with the cloud of His glory can fill us with His Holy Spirit and empower us to do His will. The same good God who did these mighty deeds can do great things in our lives.

NOTHING IS TOO HARD FOR THE LORD

Lynn de Shazo, in her great song of confession and worship, "Be Magnified," penned the words, "I have believed in a lie that You were unable to help me." The Devil would like us to think that some things are too hard for God and thereby define God in terms of human limitations. But the Scriptures state there is nothing too hard for Him.

Our God is mighty. For with God, nothing shall be impossible. What is impossible with men is possible with God. The tendency of most believers is to focus on the impossibility of something instead of its possibility with God. It is impossible for God to lie. It is impossible for Him to deny His own nature. It is impossible for Him to fail to do what He promised He would do. He can do anything. We need to put our faith in Him. As the late Pastor John Osteen wrote, "The Lord is going before me. The blood of Jesus is over me. The everlasting arms of God are under me. And goodness and mercy are behind me, following me all the days of my life."

I have often stood in front of our congregation and reminded our people of this assurance of their faith:

There is no problem He cannot solve.
There is no question He cannot answer.
There is no disease He cannot heal.
There is no demon He cannot cast out.
There is no enemy He cannot defeat.
There is no difficulty He cannot overcome.
There is no stronghold He cannot bring down.
There is no bondage He cannot break.
There is no prison He cannot open.
There is no need He cannot meet.
There is no mountain He cannot move.

There is nothing too hard for our God!

CHAPTER THREE

We Do the Ridiculous, He Does the Miraculous

And those…who believed were astonished….
For they heard them speak with tongues and magnify God.
Acts 10:45-46

In prayer one Saturday night, I heard the Holy Spirit speak to me, "Tomorrow morning in church, just pray." When I strolled into the auditorium the next morning for our scheduled pre-service prayer time, the prompting came again, "Just pray." I struggled with the suggestion since many visitors were already beginning to enter the church sanctuary. "Just keep praying," the Holy Spirit was urging.

Why are we embarrassed to do what the Lord tells us to do? Perhaps we have embraced a theology that says, "God wouldn't tell us to do anything crazy!" Often the Lord asks His people to do things that contradict rational thinking in order to move them on in faith. The thoughts of man are not the thoughts of God. He wants to position us to operate in faith, not in mere logic. He wants us to trust in Him, not in our own strength. Therefore, He might ask us to do the ridiculous. When we do the ridiculous in obedience and faith, He does the miraculous.

Believers who seek the miraculous power of God must be willing to obey the ridiculous orders of the Holy Spirit. This is true in the Old Testament stories of faith. It was also true in the life and ministry of Jesus and was seen through the early church apostles and disciples. God challenges us to obey Him when it does not make sense and that is precisely when miracles take place.

The impression grew in intensity as we were concluding our sched-uled prayer time at the start of the service. The Holy Spirit insisted I just keep leading the congregation in prayer. I argued with God, "But Lord, there are a lot of visitors in attendance today and they won't understand." He responded to my misgivings with, "Just keep praying." So, reluctantly, I obeyed—and kept on praying. Then He challenged me again and said, "Only pray one word, 'Hallelujah.'" So I began repeating the word Hallelujah. The Holy Spirit pushed me further. He said, "I want you to say 'Hallelu-JAH'" (emphasis on the last syllable). I started pacing across the front of the auditorium, with our congregation watching, saying "Hallelu-JAH" and laying my hands, in faith, on peo-ple. As I did, the power of God began to move. It was not a typical ser-vice. We tried to explain a few things at the end, read a verse of Scripture, and take up an offering, but God did more through my fool-ishness in a few minutes than I could have done through my own wis-dom in hours. I remember later asking the Lord why He asked me to do that, feeling rather embarrassed about it. Yet I knew the Lord was test-ing my obedience to His voice. I found a greater power in foolish obedi-ence than in my formal attempts to make an impression.

THE NEED FOR FAITH

If we could do it ourselves, we would not need faith! We do not need faith for the possible, but for the impossible! We do not need faith for the natural but for the supernatural! We do not need faith for the logi-cal but for the illogical! We do not need faith for the probable but for the improbable! We do not need faith for what we can do, but for what we cannot do!

In a situation that seems impossible or overwhelming, some believers give up. Some resign themselves to an old statement that I heard a lot as a boy, "If it is the will of God...." Or, in other cases, they strive until they are exhausted and try to do things in their own strength as they quote the old extra-biblical cliché, "God helps those who help themselves." But God will patiently wait until we cry out and say, "Lord, I can't do this by myself." Of course we cannot do it ourselves; we need God. Faith is dependence on God. Faith trusts Him for help. Faith believes that the supernatural intervention of God can rescue us from our circumstance.

If a miraculous healing is needed, we will only access it by faith because we cannot do it ourselves. If a supernatural provision of money is needed, we have to appropriate it by faith because we cannot pay it ourselves. If we need a solution to an apparently impossible problem, we need a divine answer that comes through faith because we cannot find it ourselves! When facing an impossible situation, we need God and He is only accessible to those who call upon Him in faith. Faith is what pleases Him.

I am confident that God does this on purpose. He allows circumstances to arise in our lives that seem to block our way. He allows enemies to resist us and cause us to call out on His mighty name. We are then faced with the timeless human dilemma: "do I try to handle this myself or do I call out on God for help?" God wants us to become heaven-dependent. If we could do the miraculous and perform the impossible, then we would not need Him, seek Him, call on Him, or give Him the glory He deserves. We would become independent and isolated from Him. Our own success would breed a stubbornness and cockiness that would eventually lead us away from the safe and eternal refuge of God Almighty.

God knows us better than we know ourselves. He knows that we need Him and He wants us to recognize our need of Him. He wants the recognition and glory He deserves. The purpose of life is not to make us look good but to make Him look good! The grand theme of earth is to exalt the Heavenly One. A primary purpose of earth-dwellers is to magnify the One who dwells in the Heavens. When He is glorified and lifted up, others are drawn to Him and become partakers of His divine nature as their lives are changed.

The very heart of the Gospel, the Good News, is to portray God's great goodness to the nations. He is the good God, with a good plan for mankind; but man, in his pride, would easily walk away from God if he were to prosper apart from Him. That is why Jesus said it is hard for a rich man to enter the kingdom of heaven. Because of his natural wealth or strength he does not think he needs God, even though his soul is spiritually impoverished. Faith is required to please God. We need it!

BIBLE BATTLES

In the Bible, no single battle was ever duplicated in exact detail. Every encounter with an enemy demanded fresh inquiry of the Captain of the Lord's hosts—requesting His permission, directives, and strategic insights for that battle. God will test our faith and dependence on Him by asking us to do something that challenges our mind and may offend our human reasoning. Consider the testimonies of Scripture.

Moses led Israel through the Red Sea and the wilderness with many mind-boggling signs and wonders including water out of a rock, bread out of heaven, and quail in the wind. He was instructed to throw a tree in a pool of water to heal it and to lift up a brass serpent on a pole to heal all who gazed at it.

Joshua followed the modeling of Moses with his own stories of obedience and faith. He encountered an angel in the plains of the Jordan, took his shoes off, and received divine strategy for taking Jericho. He led the children of Israel across the river Jordan by having the priests go into the waters first as they carried the Ark of the Covenant on their shoulders. At their first battle inside the Promised Land, the people encircled the city of Jericho for six days in silence and then, on the seventh day, marched around the city seven times. They shouted until the ground shook and the city walls fell flat. Later, one of Joshua's greatest victories was in the valley of Aijalon where God heeded Joshua's voice as he commanded the sun to stand still and allow Israel to win the battle that day.

The times of the Judges detail a history of many unusual means of defeating the Lord's enemies. Ehud delivered a secret message in the form of a dagger to an evil king's belly. Shamgar killed six hundred men with an ox goad. Jael helped Deborah by driving a tent peg through Sisera's head. Gideon led one of the most unusual battles in the Old Testament with only three hundred men against a vast army of Midianites. With a pitcher covering a torch in one hand and a trumpet in the other, three hundred commandos surrounded the Midianite camp and simply stood in place to follow Gideon's lead. They smashed the pitchers, held up the torches, blew the trumpets, and shouted, *"The sword of the LORD and of Gideon!"*[1] Their display confused the enemy and caused them to attack each other. The Israelites completely routed the Midianites without swinging a sword.

Samson showed dramatic and creative flair in defeating his enemies. He tied three hundred foxes' tails together and lit them like torches, setting the Philistine's fields ablaze. He killed a thousand men with the jawbone of a donkey. He pulled down the gates of a city and carried them into the night—posts and all. Finally, he brought down the house by pushing against the pillars inside the temple Dagon, slaying more of his enemies at his death than in his life.

King David is the first of the kings to operate under the anointing of the Lord. He set the pace for radical obedience by running at the giant Goliath with nothing in his hand but a sling and a bag of five stones. He is followed by stories of King Jehoshaphat who sent singers out in front of his army. One might surmise that if singers were leading the charge they would sing war songs or something about God's power and might; instead, he sent them out singing of the mercy and goodness of God. The resultant presence of God defeated their foes.

In all of these Bible battles, there is one constant. No matter how ridiculous God's instructions seemed to be, when obeyed they resulted in victory one hundred percent of the time. For us, life is no different. When we pray for a particular thing and God tells us that He will answer our prayer if we will follow his commands, we need to do so no matter how ridiculous the notion.

RIDICULOUS ORDERS

There is an amazing correlation between the miraculous things God did in history and the unusual commands He gave those who obeyed Him. Over and over He asked His servants to do ridiculous things in order to release His miraculous power. In addition to this, He also demonstrated His power in unusual and strange ways without the aid of man or even at times, in spite of them.

The Bible records for us the bizarre and glorious acts of God, recounting stories of burning bushes not consumed, sticks turned to snakes and back again, water turned to blood, or frogs in the bedroom. We see rivers stopped, rains released, food delivered to a prophet by ravens, a floating ax head, fire from heaven consuming enemies, and a king waiting for wind in the mulberry trees before going into battle.

The Old Testament is filled with unusual requests on God's part as

He involves His people in the miracles of the Old Covenant. Moses lifted his hands on the mountain to allow Joshua to win a battle in the valley. The prophet Elijah instructed the widow to borrow vessels and fill them with oil to receive her miraculous supply. Naaman was healed of leprosy by obeying the word of a prophet to go and dip in a dirty river seven times. Elijah and Solomon both prayed fire down from heaven. The prophet Hosea married a prostitute to model God's love for Israel, and Ezekiel was commanded to walk naked for three years to make a prophetic statement to God's people. Again, every time God's people obeyed, they received His promised blessing. The key is obedience to God's word.

THE RIDICULOUS IN JESUS' MINISTRY

In the New Testament, the ridiculous continued as Jesus opened the eyes of the blind. In the case of one blind man, He simply spoke a word and healed him. With a second, He spit in the man's eyes, and with a third He spit on the ground, made clay of it, applied it to the man's eyes, and commanded him to go wash in the Pool of Siloam. Why would Jesus do this to a man already humiliated by the infirmity of blindness?

When confronted with a tax issue, He sent Peter to retrieve tax money from the mouth of the first fish he caught. Imagine the humility it took for a fisherman like Simon Peter to go stand beside the lake that day and answer the questions of his fellows. Why had he suddenly returned to a trade that he had forsaken to follow Jesus? Why was he trying a new technique of using a line instead of a net? Why was he only trying to catch one fish? Why didn't the Lord raise His funds in a more conventional way?

Jesus' ministry was anything but predictable. He was Himself walking in obedience to His Father. Acting as He saw His Father act, He forgave one adulteress with a word but exposed another's sins by detailing the number of men she had been with. He told one rich man to just drop everything and follow Him but told another he had to sell everything and give the proceeds to the poor or else never get into the kingdom. At His first miracle, He commanded servants to fill water pots with water and serve it as wine. Later, He fed five thousand men with the lunch of one little boy who brought only enough for himself. Jesus modeled the unusual and asks of those who follow Him, the ridiculous.

THE RIDICULOUS CHURCH

The early church apostles must have caught the same Spirit of obedient faith as they came out of the Upper Room filled with the Holy Spirit. It was not long before they started jerking lame people to their feet, rejoicing when they were physically beaten by the leading officials, and sending handkerchiefs to heal the sick. Their shadow healed people. They had visions and trances in the middle of the day. Angels got them out of prisons. If angels were not enough, they had midnight worship sessions that stirred up seismic tremors, shook prisons, and brought jailers to their knees.

When the apostle Paul wrote his first letter to the church at Corinth, one of the most spiritually demonstrative churches, he told them he did not come to them with eloquent speech but with demonstration of the Spirit and power. He pointed that out so that their faith would not be in the wisdom of men but in the power of God. Because, he explained, God chose foolish things to confound the wise. He later exhorted the believers to become fools that they might be endowed with wisdom.

God still calls his followers to a life of obedience and radical faith so that their confidence will be in God and not in carnal reasoning. Would we be willing to do the ridiculous in order to obtain the miraculous? This is the exciting challenge of faith for the twenty-first century believer.

I remember attending a particular Seattle Mariners baseball game. Ken Griffey, Jr. was still in Seattle and was about to tie the Major League record for consecutive games with a home run. The old Seattle Kingdome was jammed with an emotionally charged crowd. When he stepped to the plate in the seventh inning, everyone was on their feet because they knew it might be his last chance to break the record. Griffey launched a blast over the right field fence for a home run and the dome came unglued. Fans screamed. Fireworks went off. The building rocked. Folks were hugging people they did not know. For a few brief moments, we were all lost in the magic of a game. Folks in Seattle still talk about it. We think nothing of this kind of emotional display in public and yet are often embarrassed about demonstrating our faith and freedom in church. Perhaps the Lord is restoring His Church by pouring out His Spirit, stirring our hearts afresh, jump-starting our emotions, and swinging the pendulum of zeal and passion back toward His standard of normal.

RIDICULOUS FAITH

All of this points to one thing: the major issue with God, I am convinced, is obedience. God is not impressed with our programs, sacrifices, or offerings. He has His own agenda and wants to complete it on His schedule. I think the Church has drifted. We are far removed from the days of the disciples when the Holy Spirit truly ruled their daily lives by directing their efforts toward world evangelization and the propagation of the kingdom message.

It appears the Lord is getting us back in shape. Maybe this is "Spring Training" in preparation for the big leagues. There may be more at stake than we presently realize. We may be on the verge of the last of the last days, a prophetic time period of harvest and the fulfillment the of God's covenant and purpose.

It is imperative that we learn to obey intuitively, respond quickly, and act immediately. We have to be fully submitted to His Lordship and allow Him to indeed be the head of the Church, the Savior of the Body, and the One in charge. We have to learn to respond to the gentle nudging and prompting of the Holy Ghost. So He tests us. He gives us periodic examinations. He checks our fitness for duty. He requires obedience beyond our natural understanding and outside the perimeters of our logic.

If we lean on our own understanding we will not succeed. We have to obey Him. In some regards, we need to return to the uncomplicated mentality of a first grader when Daddy and Mommy ask us to "just obey," the time that precedes those adolescent days when we tend to question why. The Church is embarking on a renewed journey of faith and trust where God asks us to do the ridiculous that we may watch Him do the miraculous.

BROTHER FAITH, SISTER WISDOM

I married an exceptional woman. It must have been a spark of brilliancy on my part for having secured such a union. Maybe not. Maybe it was the mercy, grace, and sovereign favor of God who had a wonderful plan for my life. Nevertheless, I live with this woman. Gini is "Sister Wisdom" personified. The book of Proverbs chapter seven, verse four admonishes men to make wisdom their sister and call understanding their intimate friend. No one can scan the motives of a woman like another woman. Your "sister wisdom" will save you. Do you hear her whispering in your ear? "Brother, stay away from that strange woman! I'm tellin' you, she is up to no good. Don't you be lookin' at her, just listen to me and you'll be safe!"

One summer I taught a series in our church on "Managing Your Money God's Way." Our congregation is well instructed in the Scriptures and has faith for finances. Upon every offering, we take a few minutes to exhort the church and stir their faith that as they faithfully tithe and give, the Lord will take care of them. But there are two sides to the prosperity coin. One side is faith for finances and the other side is wisdom and good stewardship with what we have. Faith does not excuse foolishness and stupidity. To exercise faith does not mean we abandon all sound judgment. It is not anti-intelligence. Faith is not ignorance nor does it ignore understanding. Wisdom is the partner of faith. The same chapter in which the apostle James describes the testing of our faith also tells us what to do if we lack wisdom. Ask of God who gives wisdom to all men liberally.

The balanced life of faith implies stepping out to do the impossible, the seemingly ridiculous, but it is not a license for foolish behavior without a foundation in reality. The reality of faith is based on the Scriptures and what the Lord has already spoken and laid down as our firm foundation. We are always wise to read, meditate on, and subsequently obey the written revelation that God has given us. Faith comes by hearing the source of wisdom, the Word of the Lord.

HE WILL DO THE MIRACULOUS

I knew it was the Lord, but I did not want to obey. It was the first Sunday in our new building and the Holy Spirit began speaking to me as I stood in front of our church during worship. I recognized His prompting, but I resisted. I heard the Holy Spirit speak to my heart, "Run around the auditorium and help the people break free from any religious spirit – Run!" I had heard funny stories about people that did such things. My grandparents had occasionally reminisced about "old time" tent meetings in which saints waved handkerchiefs and others ran the aisles. As a child, I had even seen a few dear old saints get so blessed they took off running. My discussion with God continued, "But Lord, I am the pastor. It is Sunday morning. I am all dressed up. There are visitors here." (You could probably add to my excuse list if you had been in my shoes.) I knew it was the Lord, and, after a few minutes of ego wrestling, I bolted to my left and started running the entire circumference of our auditorium, grabbing people to join me as I went. A majority of the young people joined in and before long, we had a people train. Religious spirits were defeated. The intimidation factor of a big new auditorium was overcome as the congregation abandoned themselves in praises, shouts, cheers, and celebration of the goodness of God. It sounds goofy to the natural thinking, but it liberated our people and we have never looked back in our worship.

When our pride and intellect start getting a grip on our faith, we can be certain that our loving Heavenly Father, with His perfect sense of humor, will probably ask us to do something ridiculous in order to keep us on our obedience toes. We should agree with Mary's admonition to the servants at the wedding of Cana: *"Whatever He says to you, do it"*[2] Miracles await us. The Word is near us, even on our lips. The supernatural resources of God are at our disposal. We activate those wonderful works of God through our obedience, faith, and radical trust in Him. When He speaks, we must listen and obey. If we are willing to do the ridiculous, He is ready to do the miraculous.

THE ANOINTING

I have an anointing from the Holy One. This unction teaches me all things. The Spirit of the Lord is upon me because He has anointed me. I love righteousness and hate wickedness; therefore, God has anointed me with the oil of gladness. The yoke will be destroyed because of the anointing.

My faith will not be in the wisdom of men but in the power of God and in the demonstration of the Spirit. He who supplies the Spirit to me and works miracles in my life does not do it by the works of the Law but by the hearing of faith.

God has granted me, according to the riches of His glory, to be strengthened with might through His Spirit in my inner man. I will not be drunk with wine, which is a waste; but I will be filled with the Spirit, speaking in psalms and hymns and spiritual songs, singing and making melody in my heart to the Lord. I will not quench the Spirit, and I will not despise prophecies. For God has not given me a spirit of fear, but a Spirit of power and love and a sound mind.

HE IS THE LORD OF MIRACLES

He is the God who does wonders. He is the Miracle Worker. He is the One who acts for those who wait on Him. He is the Lord of Hosts, and the Captain of them. There is nothing too hard for the Lord; for with God, nothing will be impossible. What is impossible with man is possible with God. He is the Almighty, the Anointed One, and the Creator of all things.

He opens blinded eyes, heals the leper, causes the deaf to hear, the mute to speak, the lame to walk, and the dead to be raised. Those oppressed of the evil one are healed and set free by Him. It is He who stretches out His hand and signs and wonders are done by the Name of His holy Child, Jesus.

The Seed of Abraham

Let them shout for joy and be glad, who favor my righteous cause;
And let them say continually, "Let the LORD be magnified,
Who has pleasure in the prosperity of His servant."
Psalm 35:27

When we found our first church home in Bellevue, we were thrilled to discover what seemed to be the perfect location for us to get started. Upon being informed of the lease agreement, however, we almost lost heart. The monthly rate on the space was over $8,000 a month. On a good Sunday we had one hundred people. We had very little money in the bank, yet knew that the Lord had directed us to this location. The supernatural confirmations were exceptional. As a new pastor, I discovered a foundational principle of faith for twenty-first century churches. When something is the will of God, being confirmed by two or three witnesses, God usually requires us to step out in faith before the provision comes.

Financial provision is a major need in everyone's life. We cannot live without money or some means of exchange by which our needs are provided. The writings of the apostles tell us that if a man does not provide for his own he is worse than an unbeliever. The teachings of Jesus tell us that the same God who provides for birds will provide for us. He said if we know how to give good gifts to our children, how much more does our Heavenly Father know how to give good things to us? The life of faith will always be accompanied by supernatural and tangible provision from God. Jesus said our Father knows that we have need of these tangible things. One of the clearest signs of God's favor and confirmation of His will is His provision. Because of His nature, that provision will always be abundant. Even the Old Testament Law says that obedience yields blessings that overtake us as we walk in faith. God opens the windows of heaven over us when we tithe because He blesses those who walk in obedience. When we, as His children, give, he gives back to us. What we sow, we reap. With the same measure we give, we will receive. When we give to the poor, we are lending to the Lord and He will repay. He takes pleasure in the prosperity of His servants. Whether abased or abounding, living humbly or living in prosperity, we will be blessed, prospered, and have everything we need as we walk in obedience and faith. God will see to it that we have enough in our lives to give some away and bless others.

The book of Galatians teaches us that, in Christ, we are Abraham's children. The promises that God made to Abraham regarding his children are available to all of us who are saved. We have inherited the same blessings. We receive the same eternal life that is promised. We become Abraham's children through faith in Jesus as our Savior. This is our heritage as the seed of Abraham.

BEFORE THE PROVISION COMES

We waited on the Lord. We prayed diligently for His will. We counseled with experienced men and women of faith and wisdom. We talked more. We waited longer. We thought it through. Then we prayed some more. We needed to know for sure that the Lord was directing us to sign a five-year lease that obligated us to such a large monthly financial commitment. By the deadline, our advisory board was in complete agreement. We signed a lease that required our fledgling church to pay more than $8,000 every month for the new space we so badly needed.

We have since started other outreach churches, and I am very cautious about them being obligated financially beyond what they can afford. I do not think I would recommend this business decision to anyone. Sometimes, I can hardly believe we actually signed that lease, but we did. We had three months rent-free before the payments commenced. That gave us three short months to grow, teach on tithing, and believe God for supernatural provision. I remember exhorting our small group of original shareholders on the privilege of investing in the founding of a church. They gave and God came through in glorious fashion. We never fell short financially in those first five years and even remodeled a majority of the retail area before we moved on.

In 1997, coming to the end of our lease, we needed new church facilities. Our little congregation had grown from twenty-one people to over a thousand and we desperately needed more space. The church would seat five hundred people when we squeezed and nobody breathed. It had become a special place, a true sanctuary, a place of refuge, and a temple of the Lord. In that place, God moved mightily and the Holy Spirit visited us. Many souls were saved, bodies healed, families restored, and countless lives transformed by the power of the Holy Spirit. But the time had come for a decision to be made. Would we renew our lease or move on? Could we purchase the K-Mart space that was next to us or was God going to lead us to a totally different location? We were coming to a crossroads.

During that season of praying, fasting, and seeking God for His divine direction and intervention in our situation, we felt led to invite five of the premier pastors of our city to preach at our church. They were all in the middle of their own building programs. Our local church elders made the decision to sow a large offering into each of their ministries, as a gift, to help them with their building projects. Not only did we bless the pastors with a personal honorarium for coming and speaking to our little church (we numbered about 250 adults on Wednesday nights at the time), but we also ended each evening by taking a love offering for their church. Ironically, we were the ones in greater need of finances; but believing God's Word we sowed our "seed" into their work for the harvest we so desperately needed.

SIX MIRACLE WEEKS

The pastor of the largest church in our area later told us that no other church had ever given him money in his twenty-seven years of ministry. Because of his success they never considered blessing him. He was personally overwhelmed by our faith gift. That next weekend he stood before his congregation of six thousand people and waved the check as he told the story of the little church that had given them a $10,000 offering. His congregation spontaneously erupted in applause and cheers.

We gave each of the pastors a similar offering and sowed over $50,000 into other congregations from our own city in five weeks. Within that same month, we sent $20,000 to a pastor in another nation for a new vehicle. Towards the end of that same time period another pastor (whose church had been burned down by arson) came to share his testimony and receive an offering for his church. All our hearts were deeply touched by his spirit of faith and we took up an additional $10,000 offering for his congregation.

Our church accountant reported that we had given away over $117,000 within that two-month period, including gifts to missionaries, benevolence to our own people, and other special needs. Correspondingly, our church budget did not seem to be suffering. I asked for an accounting of the surplus savings and was astounded to discover the amount to be $117,000—the exact amount we had given away.

Within two months, the Lord had funneled through our church over $234,000 of extra money above our regular budgetary needs. We could hardly believe that amazing miracle of provision. We learned a great lesson in that miraculous season of our church's history. When we had a need, we sowed a seed! The more we gave, the more we received supernaturally from God. To this day every time we take a special offering our tithes increase. The more we give away, the more our personal provision increases. The Wisdom of Solomon instructs us that the generous soul will be made rich, and, when we water others, we will be watered as well. Jesus said that when we give, *"it will be given to [us]: good measure, pressed down, shaken together, and running over"*[1]; and that with the same measure we give, it will be measured back to us.

I have taught our church family that if every member of our church would faithfully tithe and give to the Lord, we would never have a financial problem. The blessing was not on the amount of money we gave but on our obedience to His Word and His covenant. During every offering, we take five to ten minutes to exhort the people from the Scriptures and build faith for tithing and giving. At the conclusion of the first five-year period, we had paid our dues, stretched our faith, sown our seed, and the Lord had begun to open the windows of heaven to pour out a blessing we could hardly contain.

As the people were faithful in tithing and giving, the Lord was preparing His miraculous provision for our need. We were about to enter a short period of testing that ended with a blessing. We had no idea that the seed we had sown in the spring of 1997 would return to us so quickly and so sovereignly by the fall of that same year.

THE TESTING PERIOD

I will never forget that fateful Friday meeting with the landlord. It was a trial of my faith. With my associate and brother-in-law, Jerry McKinney, I had gone into the landlord's office to negotiate the renewal of our church's lease agreement. The man wasted no time in telling us that he had a better offer and we had sixty days to vacate. We had occupied that space for five years. We had sanctified and dedicated it to the glory of God. It had become holy ground to us. It was known as The City Church and The City Ministries in our community, a place where hundreds of people were being ministered to and experiencing life-changing help. We had improved much of the landlord's property and made it better than when we arrived. But he was kicking us out. I could not believe it. I politely, but emphatically, walked out of his office. I was bewildered by the hardness of his heart.

After a night of great frustration and wondering where we were going to go and how I was going to tell our people that we were now the first church of the homeless, the peace of God flooded my heart. The very next morning, at our monthly Men's Prayer Breakfast, the Holy Spirit began to speak to me. I had previously told our elders and pastors that I would not leave our location unless the Lord shut all the doors and spoke to us specifically, like He had five years earlier. The Lord was so good to us—He shut all the doors in one week. I was frustrated and wondering, but He was in total control. He even sent the same prophet, David Schoch, who had spoken an amazing prophetic word of direction to us five years earlier, to give us a fresh word of comfort from the Lord that very week.

The Holy Spirit changed my heart and opened my eyes to look at a church facility six miles to the north of us. Within seven days, after touring the building with our pastors and praying together, we signed a contract. We received confirmation through good counsel, met with their board of elders, made a generous offer, and came to a sales agreement. It was a seven-day miracle.

The building was the former facility of the six-thousand member church to which we had given a love offering of $10,000 just six months before. We had no idea that this would happen. Our bread was coming back to us on the waters of faith. When we met with their board, they conveyed they specifically wanted us to have the building because of their respect for our reputation and treatment of their pastor. God had supernaturally prepared the way and opened a great door of opportunity. When the sales agreement was announced simultaneously to both congregations, all stood and celebrated with shouts of joy. Our God *is able to do exceedingly abundantly above all that we ask or think, according to [His] power that works in us.*[2]

OPENING THE WINDOWS OF HEAVEN

We did not have a few church members who bankrolled this new project. We do not have a Millionaires or Founders club, nor did we use a fund-raising campaign or highly sophisticated program for capital investments. It was the result of uncomplicated faith, generated by the regular, public reading of the Scriptures, prayer over our offerings, every member faithfully tithing, and people giving in obedience to the Holy Spirit. God's provision kept coming through for us, month after month, like the little widow who kept going back to that miracle jar of oil and bin of flour.

Within those first six months, our people had raised almost one million dollars toward the new building. The church family gave in faith, doing their best. The Lord, in response to their faith, opened the windows of heaven, as He had promised, and poured out a blessing we could not contain. As the financial miracles began to unfold, we were left in awe of God and His goodness.

Another church in our city contacted us to inform us that they wanted to give a financial gift to our congregation. Not only did they want to bless us, but they also desired to bless the church from which we were purchasing the building. The sooner we accumulated our needed down payment, the sooner the seller would receive a large infusion of cash for the completion of their beautiful new five-thousand seat church. Our executive pastor took the message and expected a substantial gift of perhaps several thousand dollars, but we never expected what came to us by special delivery. When the courier arrived, our church was presented a cashier's check in the amount of $500,000!

A church in our own city had just given half a million dollars to us. Who had ever heard of such a thing? I called and met with that pastor, expressing our sense of overwhelming awe at their amazing liberality. Surely God was opening windows in the heavens above us and the blessings were beginning to pour down. The story keeps getting better, though.

Another couple that had recently joined our church communicated they wanted to donate a boat to our building fund. I visualized a speedboat, maybe a small yacht, but when I met them at the shipyards, we discovered a ninety-two foot fishing vessel. They had been working on the ship for years in hopes of using it for a medical mission work. Touring it, we marveled at the quality of craftsmanship they had lovingly poured into it. We stood together in the ship's salon as they carefully described to us how the Lord was speaking to them to give it to the church. I was stunned. I really did not know how to respond or if they were expecting us to take on their mission project. (I could just imagine myself in a captain's hat sailing into the steamy jungles of the Amazon and swatting at mosquitoes.) They clearly communicated that there were no strings attached and we were free to sell the ship if the Lord so directed. We joined hands in a tearful prayer, thanking God and asking for His direction. Although this couple had tried for years to sell the ship, after donating it to help build the church, it sold within three months for $900,000. We sold it to a Christian businessman who intended to use it to bless others.

Within that first year, our people raised 1.4 million dollars for the purchase of our new church facilities. The two supernatural gifts matched that amount exactly. We called it God's matching funds program.

THE PURPOSE FOR PROSPERITY

God's promise of supernatural provision for His people is directly connected to His purpose. The intent of being blessed is always to be a blessing. The prosperity has a purpose. The money has a mission. God gives faith for finances in order to accomplish His plan. Moses recorded this in Deuteronomy the eighth chapter and verse eighteen, *"it is He who gives you power to get wealth, that He might establish His covenant which He swore to your fathers."* His promised blessing on Abraham and his seed was so that, through them, all the nations of the earth could be blessed.

As the Lord begins to prosper us to get out of debt and store up extra, we need to remember it is the Lord's doing. And He who blesses intends for us to be a blessing. We are to be a pipeline, conduit, and funnel for God's blessing to others. We give people the Good News. We give people Jesus Christ. We give people hope and we give tangible blessings of goods, food, water, shelter, and clothing. The Lord's people are to be generous because He has blessed us in every area of our lives.

BLESSING THE POOR

We were also challenged by the Holy Spirit to put others first above our own needs. The first piece of property that we purchased, for example, was not a building for our church but a home for single mothers and their children. The second property was for a mission endeavor in the Philippines. As we sacrificed for others, the Lord provided for us. The apostle John admonishes us that if we see our brother in need, we are not to shut up our heart toward him but love him in word and deed by giving to help meet his need.

In the school of the Spirit we gained the understanding that when we give to the poor, we are actually loaning money to the Lord. He promises to repay as written by King Solomon in the Proverbs. Each week through our City Ministries we serve thousands of families in our community, bringing food stuffs to their apartments, homes, and institutions, as well as distributing to many other churches in our city who do the same. We give away clothing and food to anyone in need, never knowing if they are the poor or angels unawares; but knowing even when we do it unto the least of them, we are doing it unto Him!

Every Sunday, we make available a variety of donated foods and household products to our congregation and invite them to take all they want for themselves and their friends or neighbors in need. It is a practical and very effective tool of evangelism. Our goal is to equip and supply every church in our region to do the same. God wants to bless and prosper His people for the purpose of extending His rule in the earth. He has wonderful plans stored up for those who will seek Him, ask Him, and obey Him. Our heavenly Father provided for us supernaturally out of His riches in glory by Christ Jesus, way beyond what we could have asked for or imagined. He did it for His own Name's sake. He had a purpose in blessing us so that we could become a blessing to others. He is waiting to do the same for all of us!

MORE THAN ENOUGH

God promised Abraham and his seed that they would be blessed and be given an inheritance. The land of promise was given to the children of Israel but they had to possess it. It was a journey of faith that took them hundreds of years and was marked by God's supernatural provision all along the way. When the children of Israel were in Egypt, they were in bondage to Pharaoh and the Egyptians. They lived in the land of "not enough" but even there the Lord provided for them. When they left the land of "not enough" on the night of the Passover, they went out with silver and gold. The release from slavery was accompanied with great abundance and blessing.

As the children of Israel wandered in the wilderness during forty years of disobedience, God continued to provide for them supernaturally. They lived in the land of "just enough." The Lord dropped manna every morning for forty years—some 14,600 days. Bread literally fell from heaven. The Lord also provided water from a rock, a river of water gushing forth in the desert to quench the thirst of over two million people and their livestock. God also brought quail in the wind to give them meat to eat. They walked in sandals that did not wear out and wore clothing that lasted an entire generation. What incredible provision by God to meet Israel's needs for forty years.

Joshua finally led a new generation into the Promised Land of "more than enough." This was the land that flowed with milk and honey, where the grapes had to be carried between the shoulders of two men. This was the good land, a land with brooks of water, fountains, and springs that flowed out of valleys and hills; a land of grains, fruits, wine, and oil. It was a land in which they would eat bread without scarcity and lack nothing; a land whose stones were iron and out of whose hills they could dig copper. This was the land where they would not have to build the cities since houses were already constructed for them, where there were wells they would not have to dig, and vineyards and trees they would not have to plant.

The Lord wants to do the same for us today. He wants to bring us out of our poverty, that land of "not enough," beyond the place of "just enough," and into His promises of "more than enough" blessing. His desire and purpose is not only to meet our needs, but also to enable us to meet the needs of others and thereby proclaim the Gospel to our world.

As the seed of Abraham by faith, we too have an inheritance when we come to Christ. God gives us exceedingly great and precious promises through His Word. The book of Galatians chapter three tells us we are the seed of Abraham and heirs according to the promise. God delivers us out of sin and also promises to supernaturally provide for us as believers and give us an abundant life. He brings us into a spiritual heritage that gives us access to all the resources necessary to fulfill His will and purpose. That access is given by faith.

Prosperity is simply having more than enough. It is having more than we need so we can help meet someone else's need. True prosperity, of course, touches all of life and is more than just financial blessing. It encompasses our minds, emotions, health, marriages, families, relationships, businesses, time, attitudes, ministry, and finances.

Prosperity is not just about money or great wealth. It is not proof of one's righteousness or level of faith. It is not seeking money before seeking God or loving money at the expense of loving God. It cannot be measured by possessions and is not about having money at the expense of character and integrity. Prosperity is all about being a blessing to others.

OUR INHERITANCE IN CHRIST

Jesus came to take away our sins, deliver us from the Devil, heal our bodies, meet our needs, and give us eternal life—the greatest of all gifts. We have a five-fold inheritance in Jesus Christ. Every believer, in order to know who they are in Christ, must meditate on the Word of God and discover his or her inheritance. Paul tells the Ephesian Church, in the first chapter of his letter to them, that he was praying for their eyes to be opened to the riches of their inheritance. He revealed to them that the Holy Spirit was the guarantee of that inheritance. What Jesus did for us at the Cross is the rightful portion of every believer. The Bible says that at the Cross He was wounded for our transgressions and bruised for our iniquities. At the Cross He took our sins—we exchange them for His righteousness. Paul says that *"[He] who knew no sin [became] sin for us, that we might become the righteousness of God."*3 The doctrine of substitution is a glorious revelation of what Jesus has done for us. He is the Lord our Savior.

In the same way, He took our sicknesses and we take His healing. By His stripes we are healed. The stripes our Lord received on His back provide for our healing. Every disease known to man was laid on Him. He became sickness. He bore our infirmities on the tree. As Moses lifted up the serpent in the wilderness and people were healed, we also can look to Christ and be healed of our diseases and plagues. He is the Lord our Healer.

The grace of God was also manifested when Jesus became poor that we might become rich. He took the curse of poverty at the Cross that we might take His riches. We exchange places once again. Paul writes to the Corinthians, in his second letter, admonishing them to consider the grace of our Lord Jesus, who although rich, became poor so that we, through his poverty, might become rich. In the context of an extended discourse on giving and finances in chapters eight and nine, the apostle says that we can be made rich through the poverty of Christ. He also describes in Galatians the third chapter that Christ became a curse for us that the blessing of Abraham might come upon us through faith. He is the Lord our Provider. Dr. David Yonggi Cho describes this same three-fold blessing in his writings and explains how

God has provided these blessed benefits for all His children, for all the seed of Abraham in every generation.

WHY PEOPLE DO NOT PROSPER

Believers, as heirs of the promise, can fail to access their God-given resources because of a lack of the knowledge of God's Word. We are in need of a renewed biblical perspective about our heavenly Father's desired provision for His children. If faith comes by hearing, then faith to have our needs met comes the same way. Here are some reasons why Christians do not prosper:

1. We do not believe that God is a good God and that He wants to bless us (see Hebrews 11:6; Matthew 7:11; Psalm 35:27). If our image of God is that He is harsh and judgmental, it makes us reluctant to ask Him for anything. The Bible tells us that He is a rewarder of those who seek Him. If we will ask, just like a loving and good father he will help us and meet our needs.

2. We do not know or believe God's Word regarding finances and biblical prosperity (see Genesis 12:3; Hosea 4:6; Isaiah 5:13). The Bible tells us that God's people find themselves in bondage because of a lack of knowledge. Far too many believers formulate their biblical opinions without studying the Bible itself. They use their background, upbringing, and traditions to determine their doctrine, rather than the Scriptures.

3. We do not tithe or give to others (see Malachi 3:10; Luke 6:38; Matthew 23:23; Hebrews 7). Tithing was established by faith, under covenant, 430 years before the Law through Abraham and his obedience to God. The prophets confirm it, Jesus confirms it, and the Apostles write about it. Tithing is a test of our heart before God, a clear indication of where we have placed our treasure. Failing to tithe equals robbery of God and a closed heaven. If we pay our tithes and give our offerings, we will see the Lord open windows over our lives.

4. We have reacted to the extremes of prosperity teaching (see Romans 14:23). Many of us have heard exaggerated stories of

believers who have abused the teaching of the Scriptures in regard to prosperity. We often over-compensate to such a degree that we swing the doctrinal pendulum too far the other way. Instead of reaction, we should take action and search the Word of God for balanced truth. There is a wonderful purpose in biblical blessing.

5. We have not recognized "giving" as a gift of the Spirit (see Romans 12:8). Many believers have been graced and anointed by the Holy Spirit with the gift of giving. That implies that they also have the gift to get or accumulate means to give. Releasing this gift in a spirit of liberality will bring great blessing to the individual, the church, other people, and most importantly to the cause of Christ.

6. We have not used wisdom in handling our financial affairs (see Proverbs 3:13,14; Matthew 25:27; Luke 16:8). Some of us have misspent our money and incurred significant debt. We may also be reaping seeds of covetousness, stinginess, selfishness or unethical business practices. The same God who wants to give us faith for finances also wants to give us wisdom with finances. Creating wealth is a gift from God, managing it is a virtue.

WALKING IN THE STEPS OF OUR FATHER ABRAHAM

Leave your father's house and your home and go to some other country. This was the first step God asked of Abraham in his faith journey. Paul tells the Romans that Abraham was the father of all who believe and of those who walk in his steps. He is a mentor, coach, and role model for believers. He is the first fruit of faith-people. He is the prototype follower of Christ.

Reading Genesis, Romans, Hebrews, and Galatians we can learn from Abraham and begin to plot our footsteps to track in his. Try a few of these Abrahamic sandals on for size:

- We first have to leave the comforts of what we know in order to journey to the place that God has destined for us.
- All that we can see, God will give us. If we can see it (spiritual vision), we can have it.
- We cannot earn the land of promise. We do not deserve it. We can-

not work our way there. God must give it to us. It is a gift that is appropriated by faith.

♦ Miracles will come to us as we step out in faith. There are no miracles in the land of Ur. We need to get up! Go! Take action! Respond and obey. Miraculous breakthrough is just on the other side of obedience. Right on the heels of obedient faith, God's faithful and miraculous provision will come.

♦ First we step out and then comes the blessing. Abraham was blessed because he believed God and stepped out to obey, not knowing where he was going.

♦ The blessing follows obedient faith. First we believe, then we obey. Then we are supernaturally blessed.

♦ The blessing was never meant to be hoarded or self-contained. It was meant to share and give away. Abraham was blessed to be a blessing.

THE FAITH OF OUR FATHER ABRAHAM

As believers, we are children of Abraham and the qualities and blessings of Abraham can be ours. He was a great man who walked in obedient faith, commanded his children after him, trained his servants, sacrificed in worship, and interceded for others. He paid tithes of all he possessed to Melchizedek, was a rescuer of others, operated his faith on promise, not law, and was declared righteous in God's eyes because of his faith.

One of the great faith chapters of the New Testament is Paul's fourth chapter to the Romans. It delineates the steps of faith for our father Abraham. We should examine these in relation to our own lives:

1. He was made righteous by faith (see Romans 4:13). Righteousness is instantaneous through faith. We are justified by faith alone. Holiness and sanctification is a process that is determined by our obedience. It is important for us to understand the difference. Abraham demonstrated both but had righteousness imputed to him because of his faith. Righteousness grants us confidence and boldness before God and becomes the foundation for all we believe.

2. Contrary to hope, in hope Abraham believed (see Romans 4:18). Contrary to expectations of evil, Abraham held to his expectations of good. Faith is born in the womb of hope, a confident position of expecting good things. The Devil will attempt to put a spirit of heaviness upon us, causing us to become fearful and expectant of evil. We need to cast those thoughts down and expect the demonstration of God's goodness in our lives. God is a good God and every good and perfect gift comes from Him.

3. Abraham was not weak in faith (see Romans 4:19). He did not consider his own body or the deadness of Sarah's womb. We cannot focus on our own weaknesses or on the limitations of those with whom we must cooperate in order to accomplish the purposes of God. Our focus has to be on the One who is enabling us. Some day we have to quit blaming others and life's circumstances for our lack of faith and press through to do what the Lord has asked of us.

4. He was strengthened in his faith (see Romans 4:20). Reading Abraham's story illustrates how he grew in faith. His journey began in obedience, not knowing where he was going, and progressed to a willingness to give his all, his own son. At every point of testing he responded, graduating from faith to faith. He did not waver or tolerate unbelief, but was strong in faith.

5. He gave glory to God (see Romans 4:20). Abraham did not follow his own desires but the will of God. It was not his idea or a product of his imagination to find a Promised Land nor was it his idea to wait until he was one hundred years old to have an heir, only to be asked of God to sacrifice him. God was leading him, and he gave God all the glory, reserving none for himself. He took little note of himself and instead worshipped God, gave praise, offered thanksgiving, erected altars, and completely trusted the Lord.

6. Abraham was fully convinced of God's great promises (see Romans 4:21). Abraham never demonstrated a hint of doubt or an evil heart of unbelief. He was a man fully persuaded that God was going to do everything He promised. He maintained an unwavering assurance that the God who called him would perform His purpose.

7. Abraham was blessed (see Romans 4:7-9; Gal. 3:8-29; Genesis 13:2; 24:1,35; 26:12-14; 30:43). The promise God made to Abraham came

to pass and he was blessed with both favor and tangible resources. The Bible tells us he prospered greatly, became very wealthy, and possessed much cattle, flocks, servants, silver, and gold. The blessing continued to successive generations. Isaac was blessed. Jacob and his descendants to the fourth generation, through the twelve sons of Israel, were blessed. That same blessing of God on Abraham and his seed is part of the inheritance of every believer in every generation for those who live by faith.

HEIRS ACCORDING TO THE PROMISE

God is good, although some people have a difficult time receiving His goodness. We are sometimes so afraid of covetousness that we cannot receive God's blessing. We are often fearful that abundance will cause us to be corrupted. We are concerned that God's goodness will be distorted by our selfishness. He wants to bless us, do us good, and minister to our needs; but we are resistant and unbelieving. This was His promise to our spiritual father, Abraham. God blessed him that he might help, bless, and minister to others.

What we define as spoiled, God calls blessed. What we term excessive, He calls abundant. What we may think unnecessary, God knows we need before we ask. What we might call the exception, God calls the rule. What we think is undeserving, God declares to be son-ship. What we might consider begging, the Lord refers to as supplication. What may be thought extravagant, He considers excellent, and what we may feel is selfish, God does for His Name's sake. It is He who gives us power to get wealth, that He might confirm His covenant of promise. His promise is at stake, His nature is on the line, and His Word will perform what it was sent to do. He will have a people that will be blessed so that the nations of the earth might be blessed through them.

RECOGNIZING THE SEED OF ABRAHAM

I have wondered, at times, if we could actually live a lifestyle of faith like Abraham. I am convinced it would be manifest in every area of our lives including good attitude, prosperous finances, sharp appearance, diligent labor, happy countenance, positive influence, and upbeat lifestyle. I imagine others could tell it on our faces, hear it in our voices, and see it in our actions. Faith does make a difference. Faith is noticeable.

Should we judge people by their appearance or affluence? It is an obvious answer—of course not. We can be penniless, living in a one-room shack and possess genuine faith—but we will not stay there. Faith-people grow and go. Faith-people move and change, increase and multiply. Faith-people come through problems, poverty, sickness, temptation, and trials. We go deeper and grow stronger because we know the revelation of His Word is changing every part of our lives. We are the seed of Abraham and heirs according to the promise. As the seed of Abraham, we need to remind ourselves of our place.

PROSPERITY

I will remember the Lord my God, for it is He who gives me power to get wealth so that He may establish His covenant with me and through me. I am a child of Abraham by faith and therefore an heir according to the promises God made to him. As the seed of Abraham, God has promised to bless me and I will be a blessing. Those who bless me will be blessed. Through me all the families and nations of the earth will be blessed. He takes pleasure in my prosperity as His servant. He knows what I need before I ask. He will give good things to those who ask Him. The Lord God is a sun and a shield. He will give grace and glory. No good thing will He withhold from me when I walk uprightly. My God will supply all my needs according to His riches in glory by Christ Jesus.

HE IS THE LORD OUR PROVIDER

He is the God of Abraham, Isaac, and Jacob. He is Jehovah Jireh—the Lord our Provider. He is Abba, our Heavenly Father, the Bread of Life, the Creator of all things, the Heir of all things. He is Jehovah Gmolah—the God of Recompense, the Living Bread of Life, the Lord who makes all things. He is Melchizedek, the Redeemer, the Good Samaritan, the Seed of David, the Seed of the woman, the Seed of Abraham, the Blessed One, and the Great Provider.

CHAPTER FIVE

A New Breed of Faith

The LORD is well pleased for his righteousness' sake;
He will magnify the law, and make it honourable.
Isaiah 42:21 (KJV)

Every year for nearly two decades, we vacationed at a summer resort in the Cascade Mountains of central Oregon. After checking in at the fire station and paying our fees, we would proceed to the gate that led into this beautiful community. Printed on our registration card was the four-digit access code that enabled us to enter the electronically controlled gate. The numbers had to be punched before the gate would open and entrance to the community granted for our weeks of fun in the sun. No access code, no entry. No entry, no vacation. No vacation, no rest. No rest, no pastor. We needed those little numbers. The code was changed every Friday afternoon and woe to the registered guest who forgot to visit the firehouse and retrieve the new numbers. I would frequently forget, pull up to the gate as cars lined up behind us, and repeatedly punch in the wrong numbers. It usually did not take very long for the sound of car horns to reach my ears. Thoroughly humiliated, I would have to ask for mercy from other residents in order to get back into the Promised Land.

Numbers and symbols like our computer password, the access number for our voice mail, the pin numbers for our ATM card, our cell phone number, our email address, and our social security number dominate the twenty-first century. Even God has access codes! They include prayer, supplication, intercession, diligence in studying the Scriptures, and obedience to the voice of the Holy Spirit. Underlying them all is the master key of faith. All things are possible to the one who possesses faith.

Faith must be enhanced in the hearts of twenty-first century believers. It requires a fresh visitation by those who want to follow Jesus into the most exciting time of human history. The Bible defines faith and declares clearly in Hebrews 11:1, *"Faith is the substance of things hoped for, the evidence of things not seen."* Faith is substance and evidence. It consists of those things we hope for and those things we cannot see. In launching a church to bridge the twenty-first century, we discovered a simple insight into faith that changed our perspective and altered all our ministries. We do not need faith for what we can do but for what we cannot do! We need faith to believe that God can do impossible things through us.

Faith is the most powerful force in the universe because it bridges the unknown and the known, heaven and earth, eternity and time. Faith is a quality that the Apostle Paul said endures forever and is given to us as an earthly power to impact eternity.

Faith is what impelled Peter to get out of the boat and walk on water. It is the force that drove an infirmed woman to force her way through a crowd to touch Jesus' robe. It is the confidence that led Abraham up Mt. Moriah to obey the voice of God and sacrifice his only son, Isaac. It is the trust that gave Joshua boldness to possess a land promised to his fathers and the same assurance that stirred Paul to preach Christ to Caesar.

It dwells in the heart of every man and woman of God, both in the Bible and in the annals of Christian history. Faith has brought down kingdoms and raised the dead. Faith also helped Job trust in the Almighty through seasons of suffering and into great prosperity. It delivered Daniel from the lions but also kept the soul of Stephen as stones riddled his body. It anointed the apostles to plant churches across Asia, and it produced healing through pieces of cloth. Faith motivated the first generation of saints and has wrought miracles in the lives of countless believers since. It has shielded the leaders of the

Church through torture, persecution, and death, and built bridges of God-trust from one generation to another for two thousand years. The Church today needs greater faith as she navigates the uncharted territory of the twenty-first century. God is lighting a fresh fire of faith in the heart of a new generation. Faith is renewing the face of the Church.

FAITH AND THE SPIRITUAL REALM

I have only experienced a true vision from God a few times. Infrequently I have had a dream that was both remembered and significant in my life. Perhaps more rare would be the times that I believed I heard the voice of the Lord or have seen a sign in the natural world that confirmed something to me in the spiritual.

All these experiences, which must be judged and screened because of their subjective nature, nevertheless confirm the realities of biblical revelation and give us glimpses into the heavenly realm. Heaven is real and there is a great cloud of witnesses, as seen by the author of the book of Hebrews, from many generations of saints who are waiting in eternity for the culmination of history and the moment of our arrival. There is a throne that God reigns upon and Jesus sits at the right hand of. There are angels who give aid to the seed of Abraham, the heirs of salvation. And there are real demons that attempt to deceive, harass, and oppress people. When we die, our spirit will leave our body and go to a place of eternal judgment. There is a heaven and a hell. These are true biblical realities.

However, most Christians do not live as if these things are real. In contrast to the Scriptures, they live as if the temporal world of physical things is the center of creation. Faith is seeing past the visible and seeing the invisible, supernatural world of the spirit. We spend too much time focusing on the natural world and physical things. We need instead to refocus our lives on the things of the Spirit of God. There is only one way to position ourselves for faith: by building on, feeding on, meditating on, and praying over the Word of God.

THE JUST SHALL LIVE BY FAITH

Everything in the Christian life works by faith. You and I were saved by faith. We were baptized in water by faith. We received the Holy Spirit by faith along with the accompanying gifts and demonstrations of power. We attend church every week by faith. We pay our tithes and give our offerings by faith, actually believing that by giving money away our own needs will be met. We partake of the Lord's table by faith believing that the elements have more meaning than simple crackers and juice provide. We receive life, strength, healing, and renew our covenant with God by faith. We read the Bible in faith—believing that it is the infallible, unerring Word of God—and we believe that by obedience to it our lives will be better. We bow our knees in prayer because of faith, believing that a God in heaven actually hears us and will answer. We sing songs and lift holy hands, believing to be transformed into His image as we worship. We lay hands on the sick and pray the prayer of faith, expecting them to recover. We believe that by the stripes inflicted on the back of Jesus, we were healed. We believe in miracles, supernatural breakthroughs, abundant provision, the power of the Gospel, and its impact on the human heart. We believe prodigal sons and daughters will eventually come home. We believe for a great outpouring of the Holy Spirit in the last days, accompanied with a worldwide harvest of souls before Jesus returns. We believe all these things. It is our faith that has engaged these unseen realities and embraced them as real, true, and valid. This is the lifestyle we have chosen—to live by faith.

FAITH IS IN THE BIBLE

Determined to find all the Scripture verses that related to faith, I ventured into a word study. I soon discovered that all the verses of the Bible relate to faith. Faith comes by hearing the word of the Lord, and the Holy Spirit can use any verse of Scripture at any time to speak to any person in any way necessary to communicate His love. My word study did, however, produce some specific "faith facts" and insights from the Bible. There are 667 direct references to faith in the Bible, 193 in the Old Testament and 474 in the New. Jesus referred to faith and belief 156 times in all 4 Gospels (24 times in Matthew, 21 times in Mark, 25 times in Luke, and 87 times in John's gospel). The apostle Paul refers to faith and belief 192 times in his letters. The other writers refer to faith 69 times. Faith verses are found 53 times in Luke's account of the Acts of the Apostles. The epistle with the most references to faith is Paul's letter to the Romans with 50 references to faith in only 16 chapters. That averages just over 3 references per chapter. His 2 letters to his spiritual son, Timothy, are a close second with 32 comments about faith or belief in only 10 chapters. The Bible is full of faith.

This faith of which we are speaking is not just positive thinking or new age, upbeat optimism. Jesus said, *"Have faith in God."*[1] Our faith is in God who revealed Himself through our Lord and Savior, Jesus Christ. We believe in the God of the Old and New Testament, who created the heavens and the earth. He was the God of Abraham, Isaac, Jacob, Moses, Joshua, and King David. We believe in God, the Father, who sent His only Son into the world that *"whoever believes in Him should not perish but have everlasting life."*[2] We believe in Jesus Christ who died on a cross, was buried, rose from the dead on the third day, has ascended to the right hand of God in heaven, and is returning again to receive His Church. We believe in the Holy Spirit who was poured out on the day of Pentecost as a fulfillment of God's promise, who indwells the believer and empowers us to be witnesses of the resurrection. Our faith is in the living God!

Faith does not just believe in God—even demons do that. It does not just believe that the Bible is the Word of God, for even the Devil recognizes truth. Faith is more than a generic sense of reality. Faith changes the natural order. Faith generates a force, a power and an influence, that makes changes in the natural realm through the power of the supernatural. Faith is a confident trust in the power of almighty God through Jesus Christ. We do not just believe in Him, we put our trust in Him. We trust Him with our physical lives, our money, our children, and our eternal destiny.

This kind of faith saves souls, heals sick bodies, casts out demons, and provides for needs. This kind of faith can influence the weather, change the heart of a wayward child, stand strong in horrendous tests, and even alter the human personality by injecting joy, peace, and love where they did not exist before. This faith is the most powerful source of change on the planet. It comes from the Lord Jesus Christ alone. We need to open our hearts, search His Word, and read it until He speaks to us. We need to let faith have its rightful place of prominence in our hearts and lives.

WHERE IS OUR FAITH?

Jesus loves faith. He responded to faith-filled persons who demonstrated their trust in coming to Him. Just twice, though, did He commend great faith. The Roman Centurion conveyed to the Master that He need not come to his home, but simply speak the Word and his servant would be healed. Jesus was delighted with the Roman's faith, and even declared that He had not found such great faith in all of Israel. Apparently, Jesus had been looking.

A woman of Canaan came to Jesus, calling out His name and trying to get His attention. She was a Gentile woman and Greek by birth. She came boldly and begged Him to heal her demon-possessed daughter. Her faith, so amazingly resilient, overcame several obstacles to secure healing for her daughter. The disciples were bothered by her crying and asked Jesus to send her away. Initially, Jesus did not answer her cry and then publicly commented that He was not sent to the Gentiles. She, in response, worshipped Him and asked for healing for her daughter. Jesus retorted, *"It is not good to take the children's bread and throw it to the little dogs,"* referring to Gentiles. Still undaunted in her faith, she came right back, *"Yes, Lord, yet even the little dogs eat the crumbs which fall from their masters' table."* Jesus was so impressed He said to her, *"O woman, great is your faith! Let it be to you as you desire."*[3] Her daughter was healed that exact hour. Jesus gives her the highest commendation when he calls her faith *mega*-faith.

The Gospels indicate that Jesus was on a search—a "faith" exploration. He questioned His disciples: *"When the Son of Man comes, will He really find faith on the earth?"*[4] The Old Testament says the *"eyes of the Lord run to and fro throughout the whole earth, to show Himself strong on behalf of those whose heart is loyal to Him."*[5] Jesus told the woman at the well that the Father was *"seeking"* people who would worship Him *"in spirit and in truth."*[6]

When He scans our heart and searches through the recesses of our soul, does He find faith? Is there bold confidence that God can do anything? Have we embraced the assurance that He will work for us as ably as He did for the saints found in the Holy Scriptures? Has the truth of God's Word filled our inner being with conviction and boldness of soul? Has true faith been downloaded onto our spiritual hard drive and become part of the default system of our heart?

Jesus apparently went to sleep in the back of the boat after he had commanded His disciples to launch out and cross the Sea of Galilee. Sometime during the night, a fierce storm arose and began to swamp the boat. Struggling against the fierceness of the storm, the disciples began to fear for their lives and in desperation awakened the Master. *"Teacher, do you not care that we are perishing?"* He stood up in the boat (a difficult feat as it rocked), raised His hands, and commanded peace to the wind and water. Immediately the storm ceased, the wind died, and there was a great calm. The disciples, registering shock and bewilderment at what they had just witnessed, sat in amazement and stared at Him, water still dripping from their drenched garments as their mouths hung awkwardly open. Jesus confronted his dumbfounded disciples: *"Why are you so fearful? How is it that you have no faith?"*[7]

All of us can identify with the sea-soaked disciples. Jesus challenged their faith on this basis: He was the One who had directed them to cross the water, and He was in their boat. That boat, being God-directed and God-protected, was unsinkable. This is a profound lesson of faith to sustain us in the midst of our storms. The disciples were proceeding across the lake in obedience to Jesus' Word; in the same way, we need a Word from God to launch out in faith. Jesus was in their boat just as He is in us by the Holy Spirit. He is with us and has promised never to forsake or desert us. He, the Storm-stopper, Wind-controller, and Water-walker will be with us until the end of the age. This is the One who is leading our life so that we may stand firm in our faith.

Storm warnings in the natural are provided by the weather service to signal the populace and enable them to be adequately prepared. The Holy Spirit similarly will prepare us, in our faith, to weather the storms of life. He will enable us by grace and strengthen our faith to get us to the other side of our problem.

When the Apostle Paul wrote to the church at Corinth, he admonished them not to put their faith in the wisdom of men but in the power of God. Living at the center of world philosophy and education, the Greeks were famous for wisdom. Paul offended their intellect and logic with the work of the Cross of Christ. He reminded them that he did not come with eloquent words or wisdom, but instead came in demonstration of the Spirit and power of God. Where is our faith? Are we subtly deceived into putting our trust in rational arguments? Before we know it, we can slip from the realm of faith into the realm of sanctified logic or religious conceptualism. By contrast, our faith is to be in the simplicity of the Scriptures and the truth of God's Word, confirmed by His awesome power. If our daily lives are determined by precept and dogma only, with no experiential leading of the Holy Spirit, perhaps we have missed faith. If we have capitulated into a lifestyle of cold, stern fundamentalism that is void of vibrant, passionate worship and zeal, we may need to reexamine our faith. Where is our faith?

THE GREAT FAITH CHAPTER

The eleventh chapter of Hebrews has been called the great faith chapter of the Bible. (Remember that every verse of the Bible is a faith verse because God can use any portion of Scripture—any phrase, any word, at any time, with any person, in any situation—to speak by the Holy Spirit and breed faith into the human heart.) As inspired by the Holy Spirit, it has more references to faith than any other single passage in the Bible. A fresh look and simple overview of these verses can stir newfound faith in our hearts. As we re-read this section of Scripture, we will notice an outline of the characteristics of faith. Here is a paraphrased glimpse into the meaning of faith from the pages of God's Faith Manual:

+ Faith is the very substance of the things we are hoping for.
+ Faith is the substructure and foundation of reality; the steadfast courage, confidence, and assurance that what we believe is true.
+ Faith is the evidence of things not seen.
+ Faith is the proof and conviction that the invisible things of the Spirit are real.
+ Faith is what our spiritual forefathers were commended for.
+ Faith knows that the world was framed by the words of God and that the visible was made possible by the invisible.

- Faith is what pleases God, believing that He exists and is presently and actively involved in our lives or situation. Faith is diligently seeking Him, knowing that He is a good God and a wonderful rewarder of those who do.
- Faith is what motivated Abel to offer an excellent sacrifice to God.
- Faith is how Enoch pleased God and walked with Him into heaven.
- Faith stirred Noah to prepare an ark and build for the future.
- Faith is why Abraham obeyed God, going out when he did not know where he was going.
- Faith is what Sarah received to conceive in the womb of her old age.
- Faith is what gave vision to see the promises afar off and be assured of them.
- Faith is what directed Abraham to offer up the most priceless thing in his life, his own son.
- Faith is what inspired Isaac to bless his son's future.
- Faith is what moved Jacob to bless each of the sons of Joseph before he died.
- Faith is what gave Joseph confidence to plan for the departure of the children of Israel out of Egypt.
- Faith is what aroused Moses' parents to hide him.
- Faith is what influenced Moses to refuse royalty and choose affliction, to identify with the people of God rather than enjoy the temporary pleasures of sin.
- Faith is what gave Moses vision of Him who is invisible.
- Faith is the revelation that allowed Moses to keep the Passover and trust in the sprinkling of blood.
- Faith is what led the Children of Israel to follow God through the Red Sea on dry ground.
- Faith is what brought down the walls of Jericho.
- Faith is what kept Rahab the harlot from perishing with those who did not believe.
- Faith is what Gideon, Barak, Samson, Jephthah, David, Samuel, and the prophets possessed.

Through faith they:

+ Subdued kingdoms.
+ Worked righteousness.
+ Obtained holy promises.
+ Stopped the mouths of lions.
+ Quenched the violence of fire.
+ Escaped the edge of the sword.
+ Were made strong out of weakness.
+ Became valiant in the heat of battle.
+ Turned to fight the armies of the aliens.
+ Received their dead raised to life again.

Faith is what supernaturally enabled them to endure suffering and wait for the promise.

+ They were tortured; they did not accept deliverance, so that they might obtain a better resurrection. They had trials of mocking and scourging. They were enchained and imprisoned. They were stoned and sawn in two. They were tempted and slain with the sword. They wandered, were destitute. They were afflicted and tormented. The world was not worthy of them. They lived in dens and caves.
+ Faith is how they obtained a good testimony even though they did not receive the promise. They are waiting for the fulfillment of the promise through our faith. As we finish the relay race, they win the prize along with us, as part of the grand gold medal team of the ages.

So, since this great cloud of witnesses, this admirable gathering of the world's greatest believers from every generation, surrounds us, we have a clear faith-plan:

+ We lay aside every weight, every unnecessary and temporal thing.
+ We turn aside from every sin that so easily ensnares us.
+ We run our race with endurance, persistence, tenacity, fortitude, and patience.
+ We keep our eyes of faith on Jesus, who is both the Author and Finisher of our faith.

◆ We finish our course, fight the good fight of faith, and look forward to the crown of righteousness and the eternal rewards of serving Christ.

This kind of faith is still active today. Christians are living by faith and seeing miracles while others are laying down their lives for the name of Christ. Some are being miraculously delivered and still others are refusing deliverance, standing strong in faith as they are ushered into His very presence. In order for us to complete what they started, we have to do it by faith. The baton of faith has been handed off to us. We have grasped it in our hands, and we must now finish our leg of the race with confidence and total trust in a faithful Creator.

FIVE WAYS TO RECEIVE FAITH

There are five ways faith comes to every person. The Bible tells us that every person has been given a measure of faith, all can partake of a spirit of faith, all can speak the word of faith, some may operate in the gift of faith, and at specific times the Holy Spirit grants special faith.

1. Measure of faith—this is given to every person to help him or her believe in Jesus and experience eternal and abundant life. It is faith to change, repent, believe, and trust in Christ. This small measure can grow to new levels of faith as activated by the believer.
2. Spirit of faith—also known as the mindset of the kingdom, this kind of faith is available for every believer. The spirit of faith is a heart attitude that enables each of us to stay focused on our purpose for living. It helps us demonstrate the proper character of Christ and emulate what He came to do. It also assists us in maintaining a faith-filled demeanor in every circumstance.
3. Word of faith—this is a Word deposited in the heart of every Christian by the Holy Spirit. It is the confession of the believer, the way a true follower of Jesus talks. The Bible says this Word is near us, even in our mouths. We are to preach this Word, teach it, share it, and confess it, bringing hope and life to others.
4. Gift of faith—a gift of faith is given by the Holy Spirit as divine assistance to operate in great faith. This gifting is a means of great

encouragement and edification to the Body of Christ. It is the ability to believe God in the most impossible situations and trust Him for supernatural solutions. To ask for this spiritual gift opens the door to believe for other gifts as well.

5. Special faith—this allows some believers to perform unusual miracles or deeds. God granted special miracles to be done by the hand of Paul in the nineteenth chapter of the Acts of the Apostles. Pieces of cloth were sent from him to the sick and resulted in diseases being eradicated and evil spirits going out of them. The very shadow of Peter brought healing to people as they lay in the streets when he passed by. God can grant this special faith for unusual situations to accomplish supernatural things.

My friend Bob Weiner, an apostle and church planter of note in our generation, shared with our congregation several key points on the lifestyle of faith. First, he said every person has a measure of faith. Second, we exercise that faith as if it were a muscle, increasing its size and strength as we use it. Our faith is exercised on a daily basis through instant obedience to the voice of the Holy Spirit. Third, we must learn to walk by faith and not by sight, to put our trust in God's words and not in our circumstances or what we see around us. Bob explained that hope is the beginning of faith, as found in Hebrews chapter eleven, verse one. He went on to suggest a practical exercise that he uses with his young disciples. He has them write down everything they would want to achieve in life if they knew they could not fail. Those documents become the basis for the faith-dreams of those young leaders. Many of those things that are being dreamed of or hoped for become things that are believed for and brought into reality through faith.

A NEW BREED OF FAITH

There is faith and there is presumption. Knowing the difference could save our lives. Faith is not just about parting the water, walking on water, or turning it into wine. It is daily consecration to Christ, keeping the divine perspective, walking in the Spirit, meditating on the Word day and night, and maintaining godly attitudes. It is making it through the month, paying the bills, and avoiding family strife. It believes for the healing of a loved one and the provision for all the needs that arise. It is an expectation of the daily benefits He wants to load on us.

Some people wrongly assume that faith ignores the realities of life. How can we rejoice and have the joy of the Lord when life is so hard and our circumstances so horrible? How can we expect healing when our bodies are in pain? How can God expect us to be happy when we are suffering? For all these scenarios God has an answer: *"Faith comes by hearing and hearing by the word of God."*[8] Peter said that God gives us all things that pertain to life and godliness through His exceedingly great and precious promises. Because God's Word tells us to count it all joy in the midst of trials, we can do it. Because the Bible says that by His stripes we are healed, we can believe it. Because the Scriptures teach us that after we have suffered a while God will come and strengthen us, we can endure all things believing for His supernatural help. Believers are not spiritual Pollyannas who ignore life's problems. We are those who directly face the realities of life in light of Scriptures. We do battle with the sword of the Spirit. We tackle problems with promises. We stand on the legal ground of God's written Word and state our case. We are believers!

FAITH IS THE EVIDENCE

Faith is the evidence of things not seen. Faith itself is the evidence. When we believe for healing but there is no physical evidence of a change, faith is the evidence! When we believe for financial provision but there is no evidence that the money is on its way, faith is the evidence! When we are standing in faith for an unsaved loved one but there is no evidence that they are responding, faith is the evidence! When we have asked God in faith for a breakthrough but there is no evidence it is happening, faith is the evidence! It is the tangible evidence in the spiritual realm that what we are hoping for in the physical will actually come to pass.

Faith is not ostrich theology, sticking our head in the sands of spiritual fantasy and ignoring the facts of life. Faith is not running from problems. Faith is not some form of godly science, positive thinking, or optimistic confession. No, faith recognizes problems, trials, tests, and pressures. Faith discerns attacks, battles devils, and overcomes enemies, confronting them all with the living Word of God. Faith rises up in our spirit in the middle of a problem and stands strong, resisting temptation.

Faith does not hide from reality. Rather, faith addresses the reality of a problem with the higher reality of the Word. Some people put more faith in what doctors are saying than in what God says in His Word. Certain times of the year, the flu bug sweeps through our nation, passing from person to person. The doctors may predict the worst flu season ever, but we need to put our faith in God's Word and confess His promises in the face of that potential season. His Word says, *"[He] will put none of these diseases upon you."*[9]

FAITH IS SPIRITUAL

Faith is spiritual exercise. It is not something that a person can produce in the physical realm. Every person, sooner or later, must face the reality of the spiritual realm. There is a God. There is a heaven. The prophet Daniel, the prophet Ezekiel, and the apostle John did all they could in earthly terms to describe things they saw on the other side of time and space. Paul said a man was caught up to the third heaven. The first heaven is our atmosphere, the sky, and the physical universe of stars and galaxies as we know it. The second heaven is the spiritual realm where both good and fallen angels operate and the world to where all lost men will go when they die. The third heaven is where God dwells, where no evil abides and where the redeemed will go for eternity. These are the realities of eternity and the world to come. When a believer on earth, bound in this time and space capsule called life, asks for more faith to operate in the realms of the kingdom of God, he is asking for a spiritual commodity. One that will enable him to operate with confidence here (on earth) and believe in what exists there (in heaven). We cannot reduce the works of God to physical self-performed acts. They are spiritual acts. We must abide by the laws of the Spirit if we intend to enter this arena of faith and succeed.

FAITH IS A HEART ISSUE

Faith does not happen in the head. It is an issue of the heart. Paul, in his letter to the Romans, pens one of the greatest salvation passages of the New Testament. Under the inspiration of the Holy Spirit, he wrote, *"with the heart one believes...and with the mouth confession is made unto salvation."* [10] Many Christians, cerebral and heady in their approach to God and His kingdom, try and figure God out or somehow reason their way into His will. Reasoning of that kind will never produce a miracle because miracles do not operate in the realm of logic. Hebrews the fourth chapter tells us the Word of God is alive, active, and sharper than any two-edged sword, able to discern between soul and spirit. The Scriptures are a discerner of the thoughts and intents of the heart. This sword is so sharp it can slice right between the soul part of us (the head), and the spirit part of us (the heart). The Word is the means by which the believer can stay focused on faith and inhabit the heart realm.

If faith were a head thing, Peter would never have walked on water. If faith were intellectual, there would have been no Red Sea crossing or opening of the river Jordan. If we operate out of our mind only, we will never see the miraculous power of God. Although God does want us to be intelligent and full of wisdom, the Bible indicates we are not to trust in our own wisdom but in the wisdom of God. We are to *"trust in the Lord with all [our] heart, and lean not on [our] own understanding."* [11] In all our ways, we acknowledge Him and He will direct our paths.

FAITH IS DIVINE PERSPECTIVE

Perception is everything. The way a person perceives a situation will determine his or her attitude and consequent action. The Word tells us God's thoughts are not our thoughts, nor are His ways, our ways. God's ways are higher than our ways and His thoughts higher than our thoughts, like a mountain climber who ascends the heights to gain a perspective that no valley-dwellers will ever see. But we cannot scale God's peaks without faith. Only God can take us to His heights. Like David says, *"He shall set me high upon a rock."* [12] We cannot get there without His help. We cannot attain to His thinking without approaching the throne of grace every day and seeking Him. We must exercise faith. Faith gives us eagle's wings and allows us to soar high over our city, family, and situations, and allows us to look down from a whole new perspective that allows us to regain the confidence that God in us can make a difference. How quickly we forget God and fall back into the default of our own perspective. Faith is constantly seeing life from the divine perspective. Through faith, the Lord will lift us up and let us see the things that only He sees.

FAITH IS SEEING THE INVISIBLE

Faith is like "night vision" to the believer. Similar to a combat helmet on a modern soldier, we have been given a means to peer into the darkness and walk securely by faith. Thomas said to the other disciples that he would not believe until he personally put his finger into the nail prints and the wounded side of Jesus. But when Jesus appeared, he did none of that, instead calling Him Lord and God. Jesus then declared to Thomas, *"because you have seen Me, you have believed. Blessed are those who have not seen and yet have believed."* [13] We worship the God who is *"immortal, invisible...who alone is wise."* [14] Through faith we see things the unbelieving cannot see.

FAITH IS BEING OBEDIENT
WHEN WE DO NOT FEEL LIKE IT

Many well-meaning Christians succumb to their feelings because they do not want to "fake" life. The Scriptures teach the believer to operate in faith. We are not to fake it, but rather faith it. If the Bible says we can do something, or we should do something, then we do it whether or not we feel like it. In fact, to press through emotions and carnal impressions and live in faith will often release us into a new realm of satisfaction in God. When worshipping, I do not always feel like raising my hands and singing, but the Bible says it is a good thing to do, so I do it by faith. The reward is His presence. I rarely feel like bending my knees and praying in the morning, as God's Word teaches, so I do it by faith. The reward is His grace. The hardest part of meditating in the Word of God daily is opening my Bible, but I do it by faith. The reward is success. If I share the Gospel with unbelievers, people will get saved. If I tithe on my finances, the windows of heaven will open and supply all my need. All these promises and more will work when we act on them by faith, regardless of our feelings. A quote attributed to Martin Luther has long been an encouragement to me: "Feelings come and feelings go and feelings are deceiving. My warrant is the word of God, nought else is worth believing."

FAITH IS FEARING HIM MORE THAN MAN

King Solomon wrote, *"the fear of man brings a snare, but whoever trusts in the Lord shall be safe."*[15] Someday, every believer must cross a line in the Spirit and no longer fear the faces of men. Fear of men's opinions brings bondage. What God thinks must always be more important to us than what people think. If we are constantly afraid of what people think, we will never do anything significant for God. Imagine the outcome if people like Daniel, Esther, Job, or King David had yielded to the fear of man. What a tragedy it would have been! The faith-filled person is so in awe of God and the Lord so real to him that men pale in comparison and stand no chance of having equal influence regarding the decisions of the heart.

FAITH IS STEPPING OUT BEFORE THERE ARE STEPS

If Peter had waited until a pathway in the lake appeared before stepping out onto the water, he would still be in the boat. He climbed out of the boat on the command of Jesus to *"Come."*[16] Faith is stepping out before there is a stepping stone. Faith is giving before we have any assurance that a return is on its way. Faith is speaking out the word of knowledge and praying for the person before there is any evidence of healing. Faith is making the plans to purchase the building before we have the money to buy it. It was the motivation behind Abram leaving Ur of the Chaldees, behind Noah building an ark, and behind James and John leaving their nets to follow Jesus. Our job is to step out, His job is to provide the pathway.

FAITH IS HOLDING STEADY IN CONTRADICTION

When walking through the valley of the shadow, we need to know that the light of His Word will enlighten our pathway. When encountering obstacles and opposition to our God-given goals, we need to know how God's mountain-mover works. When feeling the heat of a trial, we need to have confidence that we are going to come out like gold. When faced with the confusion of contradiction, we need a compass of faith to keep us on course. When circumstances and timetables do not seem to be working in our favor, faith will hold us steady. We need to run our race with endurance. Through faith and patience we inherit the promises. We need endurance that after we have done the will of God, we will receive the promise. Paul tells the warriors of Ephesus, *"having done all...stand."* 17 Pastor Leonard Fox, a wise and seasoned prophet from southern California, exhorted young preachers by saying, "the way to make it a long time in the ministry is don't quit." It is always too soon to quit. We must persevere! Our promises await us.

FAITH IS VISION BEFORE PROVISION

If we wait until it works into our budget, we will never step out to do what God is asking of us. If our vision is truly from God, then the Author of our vision is also the Financier of our provision. Believers who are waiting for the prosperity before they give have it backwards. The Bible indicates that first we give, then the blessing comes. First we sow, then we reap. If we obediently honor God with our firstfruits, He will open the windows of heaven and supply all our need according to His riches and glory. Faith declares that God-birthed vision is a priority of heaven and we are not qualified to worry about the supply.

FAITH IS A SECRET LANGUAGE

A faith-filled person is easy to recognize. They are fluent in a classified language that includes a distinctive confession. Their conversation is on a higher level. No, this is not a foreign language of some lost tribe, nor is it the gift of tongues that is described in the Bible. This is the language of God. It is the language of His Word. It is the vocabulary of the Scriptures. It is the language of faith. Faith utilizes the Spirit and words of God to dominate and control the direction of the tongue. The tongue, like the rudder of the ship or the reigns of a horse, can guide the life of a believer into favor and success.

FAITH IS TAKING AUTHORITY

God gave man dominion over the works of His hands, commissioning him to have authority over the earth and subdue it. Jesus gave His authority to His disciples: *"all authority has been given to Me in heaven and on earth. Go therefore..."*[18] We have authority over the works of the Devil, over sickness and disease, over demons and evil spirits, over poverty and lack, and over sin and temptation. We can resist the Devil and confront evil spirits that attack us or our families, standing up against the Devil and his feeble plots. We must take the authority that has been given to us and fight the fight of faith. Faith is taking authority to enforce the victories of the Cross. We are to take responsibility for our spiritual growth. It is not just the pastor's task or the church's role to bless us, promote us, or release us. It is our faith and obedience that causes these things to come to pass. We need to take the initiative.

FAITH IS FULFILLING GOD'S DREAM

The Lord took Abraham outside his tent, and showed him the stars of the heavens, and said, *"So shall your descendents be."*[19] The Scriptures tell us in four different places that Abraham believed God and it was counted to him for righteousness. Faith is always tied into God's ultimate purpose, which is the redemption of mankind. God loves people. Faith works by love. God is not willing that any should perish but that all should come to repentance. Faith sees people repenting and coming to Christ. God wants all men to be saved and come to the knowledge of the truth. Faith believes the dream of God—that multitudes will be saved and become His children. The lifestyle and passion of a man or woman of faith will be congruent with the great commission, the grand plan of God—the winning of souls. The final purpose of faith, here on earth, is to believe in the power and love of God, to boldly share the Good News of Jesus Christ, and take as many people to heaven with us as we can.

FAITH IS ACTION

- Noah had to build and prepare the ark for the coming flood (see Genesis 7:5).

- Abraham had to leave his father's house and go to a land he had never seen (see Genesis 12:4).
- Moses had to stretch out his hands on the mountaintop throughout Joshua's battle in the valley (see Exodus 17:11).
- The widow had to bake a meal for the prophet before her provision came (see 1 Kings 17:13).
- Naaman had to go and dip in the Jordan seven times to be healed (see 2 Kings 5:10).
- Esther had to boldly go in to the king's presence before God gave her favor (see Esther 5:2).
- David had to face the giant for the Lord to deliver him (see 1 Samuel 17:48).
- King Joash had to strike the ground with the arrows, but God gave the victory (see 2 Kings 13:18).
- The woman with the issue of blood had to reach out and touch the hem of Jesus' garment (see Matthew 9:20).
- The servants had to fill the water pots with water before the water turned to wine (see John 2:7).
- The ten lepers had to make their way to the priest to be healed (see Luke 17:14).
- The blind man had to go and wash in the pool of Siloam to see (see John 9:7).
- Peter had to go to the lake and catch the fish with the coin in its mouth (see Matthew 17:27).
- The four men had to open the roof to let their sick friend down at Jesus' feet (see Mark 2:3).
- The 120 in the Upper Room prayed and waited, and God poured out His Spirit (see Acts 2:1).
- Peter did the preaching at Cornelius' house and God visited the Gentiles (see Acts 10:21).
- The people had to position their sick family members on the roadway so that the shadow of Peter could fall on them for healing (see Acts 5:15).
- Paul and Silas had to sing and pray in the Philippian jail so that God could shake the building and deliver them (see Acts 16:25-26).

At some point, we are going to have to do something, take some action, step out, and get serious about exercising our faith. Batteries not included. Some obedience is required!

FAITH

God has given me a measure of faith, which is the substance of things hoped for and the evidence of things not seen. I will please God, because I believe that He exists and that He will reward me when I diligently seek Him. For whatever is born of God overcomes the world. And this is the victory that has overcome the world, even my faith.

If I have faith as a mustard seed, I will speak to mountains and they will move, and nothing will be impossible for me. All things are possible to me because I believe. Lord, I do believe; help my unbelief! I will have faith in God. I will fight the good fight of faith.

NOTHING IS IMPOSSIBLE

Jesus is the Author and Finisher of my faith. There is nothing too hard for the Lord our God. For with God nothing will be impossible. What is impossible with man is possible with God. There is nothing too difficult for Him. He is the Mighty One of Israel.

CHAPTER SIX

How Faith Works

Remember to magnify His work, of which men have sung.
Job 36:24

We live in a fallen world. The creation has been subjected to futility in the hope that a remnant of believers would rise in faith and be the agents of deliverance. All are waiting for true sons and daughters of God, who walk in overcoming faith, to be revealed.

Tests, trials, and temptations come into everyone's life. Problems, calamities, crises, and difficulties challenge us all. Obstacles, stumbling blocks, bumps, and bruises stand between our destiny and us. Devils and demons, imps and fiends fight and resist. Hindrances, hurdles, and hassles abound. Detours, distractions, dilemmas, and delays; predicaments, pickles, and fixes lay in everyone's path. Life is full of trouble. Only faith, and a sincere trust in God, can rescue us. Faith is life's only answer, in that it is man's only chance to access the supernatural power of God to intervene in degenerate situations. Bad things happen to good people. Evil is real. The Devil is alive and active on the planet. Chaos rules the powers of nature. Disease attacks young and old alike. Disaster can strike at any moment. This is the nature of the world in which we find ourselves, a world whose only remedy is faith in God. Our faith must rest in a God who rules over creation, dominates demons, and can divinely intervene to perform impossible and miraculous feats that re-create, heal, help, deliver, and rescue fallen mankind.

How do we operate in this kind of faith? How do we grow in faith? How do we learn the bold faith and access the divine storehouses of the miraculous? We all need a genuine and effective faith, founded solidly on the revelation of God's Word and accompanied by an inward knowledge of who He is. We need faith for healing, salvation, provision, reconciliation, strength, peace, or wisdom. Faith has an answer for every human dilemma. Faith is not complex, although it is not always easy.

Everyone will experience physical sickness, weakness, or disease at one time or another and be in need of faith for healing. We all have loved ones or friends who are without Christ and need to be saved, or prodigal sons and daughters who need to return to the Father's house. Financial obligations and responsibilities will require faith to trust Him for abundant provision. Offenses necessitate faith on our part to make things right with others. Stress and anxiety demand faith in order to secure peace from the Lord. Every believer needs the mind and wisdom of God to make good decisions and determine the will of God in daily situations. So how does the believer grow in faith? How does this faith work? There are some simple steps involved in generating greater faith.

WORD

We must read the *logos* until we get a *rhema* (see Romans 10:17)! Hidden in the pages of the Bible (Greek word *logos* or the written Word of God) is our answer. It is not Bible reading alone that will breed faith, but receiving a *rhema*-word (Greek word *rhema* means the spoken Word, or the Word that is proceeding out of the mouth of God) as you are reading the *logos* Scriptures. Faith is engaged when we receive that rhema-word from God. *"Faith comes by hearing, and hearing by the [rhema]-word of God."*[1] Solomon said if we seek for wisdom like it was gold and hidden treasure, then we will find the knowledge of God.

A father gave his son a Bible when he sent him off to college. After a few weeks, the son called his Dad needing money. The father asked him if he had been reading his Bible. The son alleged he was too busy but promised to start. The Dad encouraged him if he would just read the Word of God that the Lord was sure to provide. After a few more weeks of financial struggles, more calls home, and borrowing money from friends, the young man, in desperation, opened the Bible his Dad had given him and began to read. There in the pages of the Bible the son discovered twenty-dollar bills tucked tightly into the binding of several pages. His provision had been there all along, but he had not taken the time to search for that hidden treasure. Better than money and more precious than gold, our *rhema*-word is waiting for us. We need to keep reading. Keep searching. Keep meditating. God's perfect instructions and leading will come just when we need it.

Desperate for a word from God in November of 1991, I sought the Lord and He spoke to me through the Scriptures by specifically directing me to start a church in Seattle, Washington. That same precise guidance can be ours as we seek God's will for our own personal lives.

TRUST

We need to trust in the Lord with all our heart (see Proverbs 3:5)! After receiving a *rhema*-word from the Lord, we must believe it. It is with the heart man believes, Paul says to the Romans. We have to trust the Lord with our heart and not try to figure it out in our head. Remember, it may seem ridiculous, but if it is from God it will have miraculous results.

When I heard the Lord speak to me in 1997 to go buy our new building, it did not make sense because we did not have the money. But I knew it was God and had the confirmation of His inner peace. We believed. We trusted Him with our hearts, not our heads, and we received what He said we could have. If we will exercise faith when the Holy Spirit speaks to us, the Lord will guide us.

OBEY

Whatever He says, we must do it (see John 2:5)! We must take action once the Lord has spoken to us. There will always be a demand with the command. He will direct us. He will speak to us. He will enable us, but we must respond in obedience. We cannot hesitate. Like the old Nike slogan promoted, we should "just do it!"

When we signed a lease/purchase contract for a huge church facility within seven days of deciding to move out of our rented storefront auditorium, it was an amazing miracle and a bold step of faith. The new building was priced at eight million dollars and we had no millions of dollars. But within one year of signing that contract we raised, with the help of the Lord, nearly three million dollars and purchased the building. The next year we paid off another million dollars on our mortgage. He told us to do it, so we did it. We exercised our faith, and He came through with the miracle provision. He will do the same for all of us, but He requires our obedience.

CONFESS

We must confess by speaking the Word of God to our situation (see Romans 10:8-10; James 3:2; Proverbs 18:21; Mark 11:23)! Our tongue is the steering wheel of our life. James illustrates it as the rudder of a ship and the reigns of a strong stallion. Solomon spoke about the tongue in the Proverbs, writing that death and life are in the power of the tongue. Jesus said we would be justified or condemned by our own words.

We need to declare the Word of the Lord to our mountain, our problem, and see it removed by faith. Jesus told us we could have whatever we want if we believe and do not doubt in our heart. The word of faith is near us, Paul told the Romans, even in our mouths. It is that word of faith that we are to speak out boldly.

After hearing from God, with the confirmation of many credible witnesses, we told everyone who would listen of our dream for a church in the Seattle area. We talked about what kind of church we would have, and today we have that kind of church. If our words line up with God's Words and revelation to us, we will have whatever we say.

REWARD

He is a rewarder of those who diligently seek Him (see Hebrews 6:12; 10:36; 11:6)! God is so good. He is so faithful. He will not only call us, He will do it. He not only starts good works in us, He completes them. We should expect fruit and results. With God, things always *"work together for good."*[2] *"No good thing will He withhold from those who walk uprightly."*[3] If we have obeyed in faith, He is pleased and we can fully expect a marvelous reward.

Those that have the biggest smiles on their face when we retell the stories of The City Church are people who followed us and participated in the miracle. They were there. They believed. They received. They gave and they have their reward. God's plans for us are far beyond what we can imagine and they necessitate a position of faith and trust in His good reward. If we sow seed, we will reap a harvest. We must expect it! The reward is on its way.

DO NOT BE DECEIVED

The only problem with being deceived is that we do not know it. Deception is subtle. It is a trap. But the Word of God will keep us from deception. Jesus warned His disciples four times in the context of describing the end of the age to beware of deceivers. A hallmark of the last days will be deception and perversion of truth. Men will love themselves more than God, and they will have forms of godliness but deny the power of it. Sincere faith is the only answer to those wanting to escape the corruption of the world and sin's deceiving ways.

Deception is a snare to those weak in faith and to those who are looking to avoid truth. People steer clear of truth when they do not want to obey it. Truth is costly. If we believe in the reality of sin, then we are forced to consider repentance and some kind of Savior. In order to reject truth, we must formulate an alternate source of belief. We must create a lie.

The story is told of two university sociology classes that were taught by the same professor. In one class, he taught that it was possible for an untrained person to successfully work with the mentally handicapped. When making the same statement to the second class, he also presented the opportunity to volunteer at a local institution. The first class believed his teaching without rebuttal, but the second class disputed his conclusions. They did not want the responsibility of having to volunteer at the institution. They rejected his precept because it would have cost them something. Truth will cost something. It is expensive. It demands action. We must relinquish the control of our lives to our Creator. Our quality of existence depends on what we do with truth.

Other people believe a lie because they do not know the truth.

People do not know the truth because they do not read their Bibles. The truth alone does not set us free. We must know the truth and the truth we know will set us free. Knowledge of the truth and obedience to it is what saves people. When we know the truth, the truth will make us free.

Willfully ignorant people choose to believe a lie by ignoring the truth. Unchecked and inordinate desires or a wrongful lust to acquire or achieve something can mislead. Interpreting the Scriptures to our own advantage by ignoring portions that confront or convict, while at the same time embracing others that seem to confirm our selfish desires, will lead us into deception. We will find ourselves hunting for license verses and avoiding lethal ones. We will search for carnal revelation and reject spiritual revelation. If we do these things we are in danger. We are compromising. We are drifting. We are backsliding. We are transgressing His commands. We are missing the mark. We have a bent toward iniquity. We are not operating in faith, but selfish unbelief. We are in trouble.

Do you struggle with faith in God? Have you rejected truth because it scared you? Have you been running from God because you wanted to maintain control of your own life? Faith is your way out of trouble. It is time to turn around and embrace the sweet truth of the love of God. His mercy is everlasting. His truth endures to all generations. His truth is here for you now. His truth can set you free. Jesus said, *"I am the way, the truth and the life. No one comes to the Father except through Me."* 4 You must turn from deception and lies and trust Him today. You need to put your faith and trust in the One who made you and knows you. He can bring order and purpose to your life. If you have never been born again, you can experience Him now. You can invite Christ into your life today.

A man of Ethiopia, a eunuch who had great authority under Candace, Queen of the Ethiopians, was riding in his chariot on his way back to his homeland from Jerusalem. He had been to the Holy City to worship and while traveling home was reading the prophecy about Jesus from the prophet Isaiah that said, *"He was led as a sheep to the slaughter."* Under the leading of the Holy Spirit, the evangelist Philip approached him and asked him if he understood what he was reading.

He responded, *"How can I, unless someone guides me?"* Philip started with that Scripture and preached Jesus to him. The Eunuch, upon seeing water, asked if he could be baptized. Philip voiced, *"If you believe with all your heart, you may."* The eunuch instantly answered, *"I believe that Jesus Christ is the Son of God,"* and so Philip baptized him. [5]

If you believe in your heart that Jesus Christ is risen from the dead and He is Lord and God, then pray this prayer out loud and make a verbal confession of your need for Him.

> *Heavenly Father, I believe in you and in your Son, Jesus Christ. I believe that Jesus died for my sin and was raised from the dead to give me life. I ask you to forgive me and cleanse my heart from sin. I invite you into my life to be my Lord and my Savior.*

If you prayed that prayer in sincerity and truly believe these things in your heart, you are a new creation in Christ and now part of the family of God. The Lord will honor your simple trust in Him. You have become a new person. This is just the beginning of your faith journey.

LEVELS OF FAITH

When a person first comes to Christ, it only takes that small seed of faith planted in their heart to bring about spiritual change. The Bible says we become a new creation. It is like being born again—born of the spirit, not just of the flesh. Our spiritual person was dead, but now it is alive through Jesus Christ. Like a caterpillar that emerges from its cocoon, we have been transformed. Our salvation has become the foundation for growing faith.

Everyone comes to God at some level of faith and every man has been given a measure of faith. According to Romans the first chapter, where the apostle Paul is describing the power of the Gospel, he writes that *"the righteousness of God is revealed [in the Gospel] from faith to faith."*[6] There are levels of faith. A desperate father came to Jesus with his mute son and begged, *"If You can do anything...help us."* Jesus answered, *"If you can...all things are possible to him who believes."* In weakness and with tears he confessed his need, *"Lord, I believe; help my unbelief!"*[7] In response to his faith, Jesus delivered his son from that demonic influence. This man made a humble and honest declaration of his lack of faith.

Our faith should increase from the level we are at today to new levels of trust in God. As the apostle Peter described it, we should *"grow in the grace and knowledge of our Lord and Savior Jesus Christ."*[8] There are ten levels of faith listed in the Scriptures:

1. Weak Faith—the word means "to be feeble and without strength, powerless, needy, or sick." This is the beginning of faith for most (see Romans 4:19; 14:1).
2. Lacking Faith—Paul prayed for the Thessalonians that what was lacking in their faith might be provided for them. The Greek word points toward a deficiency of resources; poverty, lack, or destitution (see 1 Thessalonians 3:10).
3. Little Faith—this word carries the meaning of "trusting too little." We have moved from infancy, but are still toddlers in our faith. If we still struggle with doubt, we are at the level of little faith (see Matthew 16:8; 14:31).
4. Seed Faith—at this level, faith can now produce something. The word used here for seed means grain, such as a seed of wheat or corn. This seed is powerful and holds the potential of a full-grown plant or tree (see Matthew 17:20).
5. Increasing Faith—we now enter the levels of faith where growth is evident. This word literally means to "cause to grow or to increase," and it is used of plants, infants, multitudes of people, or of personal Christian growth. We are only half way there and must keep growing (see 2 Corinthians 10:15).
6. Exceedingly Growing Faith—Paul commended the Thessalonians for their growing faith. He uses a word in the Greek language that means to "grow beyond measure." It is the same word as level five, but with the Greek prefix *huper.* We would use the word hyper, meaning something super, extra, or special. Now we are really growing in our faith (see 2 Thessalonians 1:3).
7. Rich Faith—an incredibly descriptive word meaning, "abounding in resources, abundantly supplied, or abounding in virtues and pos-

sessions." This level of faith abounds in the wealth of the kingdom of God (see James 2:5).

8. Strong Faith—Abraham had this kind of faith. The word means to be "endued with strength." Now we are graduating to a level of faith that has endurance in its mix. This is where faith becomes invincible (see Romans 4:20).

9. Great Faith—there were only two people in the Scriptures who were commended for great faith. They were both foreigners to the nation of Israel, one a Roman centurion and the other a Syro-Phoenician woman. They both impressed Jesus with their resilient faith on behalf of another. Great faith is usually mobilized on the behalf of others. There are two definitions of great faith. The Greek word used in reference to the Roman centurion described faith of "great quantity." In regards to the amazing woman whose daughter was delivered from a demon, a much stronger Greek word is transliterated, mega, meaning "greatest in intensity, extent, stature, rank, authority, and power; of great importance or excellence" (see Luke 7:9; Matthew 8:10; 15:28).

10. Perfect Faith—the Apostle James describes perfect faith as belonging to one who is a doer of the word and exercises faith to change. It means to "complete something or to carry through thoroughly; to bring to an end; accomplish and fulfill." It is not enough to just confess faith. The definitive test is the doing and performing of it, demonstrating faith in real life situations. This is faith that is tested, perfected, and matured. This is our ultimate goal (see James 2:22).

We can grow from weak faith to strong faith, from little faith to great faith, from lacking faith to rich faith, and from seed faith to perfect faith in the process of fulfilling the incredible destiny that the Lord has planned for our lives.

INNOCENCE—THE SOIL OF FAITH

Jesus told His disciples that unless they were converted and became like little children, they could not enter the kingdom of heaven. Referring to children, He also said, *"Of such is the kingdom of heaven."*[9] I believe that childlike innocence is the ground for cultivating great faith in God. Innocence is a remarkable quality we tend to lose some-where between childhood and adulthood. Jesus told His disciples that unless they became like little children again, they could not even enter the kingdom of heaven. Innocence is at the very soul of child-likeness. It is that sweet and simple quality that we see in a teenager when they are not trying to impress their friends. Although now in a grown-up body, they revert momentarily to being a child, a glimpse of former naiveté that we wish we could freeze-dry. Every parent wishes they could preserve that innocence of childhood that is so quickly replaced with sophisticated adult activity.

It is so easy for a child to believe. Some might call it gullible, but I think of it as innocent faith. A child believes Dad and Mom can take care of everything. They are carefree and optimistic. They totally trust with an innocent faith.

Here are five childlike traits that will generate a stronger faith:

1. Purity—which breeds a holy faith. Keeping our hearts pure before the Lord is that which gains us entrance into His presence. It is this uncontaminated purity of spirit that allows faith the environment in which to thrive.
2. Authenticity—which produces a sincere faith. A person who is gen-uine, transparent, and honest will provide the richest soil for the seed of the Word of God in which to flourish. The Lord wants His commandment to produce love out of a sincere faith.
3. Simplicity—which creates a straightforward faith. The Gospel mes-sage is simple and uncomplicated and is to be preached in a man-ner comprehendible to all, including the poor, the uneducated, and the illiterate. Faith comes by hearing, not reading. No doctrine should be so heady and complex that it robs people of their faith. We must safeguard the sweet simplicity that is found in Jesus.
4. Expectation of good—which releases a positive faith. Everything always works out in the mind of a child because Mom and Dad will somehow make it better. Similarly, our good heavenly Father makes everything work together for good for those who love Him and are called according to His purpose. Even bad things turn around for our benefit. This is divine optimism. This attitude, coupled with

thanksgiving, will make us both popular people as well as faith-filled followers of Jesus.

5. Joyfulness–which engenders a happy faith. Children do not spend a lot of time being sad. They quickly rebound emotionally. Child's play is their source of fun and work. God wants His children (that would be you and me) to play more, enjoy His presence, and not get so overwhelmed by the cares and concerns of life. Most Christians are often too intense. Someone brilliant said, "Life is much too important to be taken seriously." Go ahead. Enjoy life. Be happy.

FAITH OF A CHILD

We were vacationing at my mother-in-law's house in Sacramento, California one summer. Gini's mom, Yvonne, had just walked in the door with an armful of groceries and appealed, "Wendell, there is a dead bird at the front door, would you take care of it?" I went directly to the door, partly out of curiosity (since I am a bird watcher of sorts) and partly out of duty. My daughter Wendy, about age five at the time, followed me out. What I found was amazing. A tiny violet-colored hummingbird had apparently flown into the windowpane and was lying there on the front porch. I picked it up in my hand and took my first close look at one of God's most beautiful creations–the tiny, feathered helicopter of the bird kingdom. Small enough to fit into my palm, both Wendy and I were fascinated by its beauty and size. It appeared dead and did not respond as we touched it. I asked, "Wendy, do you think God can heal this bird?" She responded enthusiastically, "Yes, Daddy." I said, "Let's pray for it." We both laid a finger lightly on that cute, miniature creature and prayed a simple prayer of faith in the name of Jesus. I am not sure I expected what happened next. To our amazement and shock that tiny hummingbird sat up in my hand, looked around, engaged its wings in motion, hovered for a split second over my hand, looked at us as if to say, "Thank you," and then darted off into the afternoon sky. I was stunned. Wendy burst into squeals of joy and ran back into the house to tell everybody the story of the bird that came back from the dead. Such is the faith of a child and such can be ours.

FAITH THAT OVERCOMES

For whatever is born of God overcomes the world. And this is the victory that has overcome the world, even my faith. I will fight the good fight of faith and lay hold of eternal life. I will not become sluggish, but I will imitate those who through faith and patience inherit the promises. I will draw near with a true heart in full assurance of faith. Therefore, since I am surrounded by so great a cloud of witnesses, I am laying aside every weight and the sin which so easily ensnares me, and I am running with endurance the race that is set before me; looking unto Jesus, the Author and the Finisher of my faith.

HE IS THE REWARDER

We have faith in God who is the Alpha and Omega, the Author and Finisher of our faith, the Bishop of our souls, the Everlasting Father, our Exceeding Joy, the Express Image of His person, our Faithful Creator, the Faithful Witness, our Foundation, He who has the key.

He is the I AM, the Bread of Life, the Door, the Good Shepherd, the Light of the world, the Resurrection and the Life, the Son of God, the Vine, the Way, the Truth, and the Life. He is the Lord who is faithful, the Power of God, the Living Word of God.

CHAPTER SEVEN

The Enemies of Faith

O LORD, behold my affliction: for the enemy hath magnified himself.
Lamentations 1:9 (KJV)

December of 1996 was a record month for rainfall in the Northwest with floodwaters rising across our region. Rivers overflowed their banks, people were driven from their homes, and sinkholes appeared in the middle of highways. No picturesque snow, just torrents of non-stop falling rain. It was a depressing holiday season.

It was also the darkest days of my ministry. I was struggling with my faith, doubting my doctrine, and wrestling with the spirit of unbelief. We had just lost the third of three precious members of our church to cancer. All three were too young to die. All three were filled with faith. All three went to heaven within a few months of each other. We prayed and fasted and cried out to God for them, but all three died. We buried one in July, a second in November, and the third just three days after Christmas.

I was the pastor of a church that believed in divine healing. We put our trust in the Lord our Healer. We practiced healing in our services and saw many people touched by the power of God. Yet there was an obvious contrast between the healing ministry of Jesus and the power level in our church. Our church hungered for more of the healing virtue of God to be manifest in our meetings and in the lives of believers.

My confidence challenged and my prayers not working, I fought a heavy battle for my faith. I heard the voice of the Devil in my ears challenging my actions, ridiculing my faith, and mocking my theology. He barraged my mind with doubt and unbelief and lied to me saying people would become discouraged and leave our church. He railed against me saying that my faith did not work and that I might as well give up. I learned that week that if we were going to exercise faith, we better be ready for it to be challenged and tested. There is a devil, we live in a fallen world, and the flesh is weak. Unbelieving spirits are bound to withstand our faith and attempt to dishearten our walk in Christ.

SINKHOLES AND THE DEVIL

I got sick and tired of the flooding. I got tired of seeing nothing but pouring down rain and dark gray clouds. I was angry that three of our beloved people had died. So I called my cousin Ken Wilde in Boise, Idaho and asked him to pray for me. Ken, the pastor of one of Idaho's greatest churches, Capital Christian Center, is my family, friend, and, in this case, also my counselor. He began to describe what others have called the dark night of the soul. As he talked about this kind of depressing circumstance that people often find themselves in, I began to weep. I remembered how, in many of the Psalms, David cried out to the Lord as he struggled with the humanness of his soul. I cried out to the Lord as Ken prayed for me. That week my captivity was turned and the floodwaters of my soul began to subside.

I got mad at the Devil and came out swinging. I felt like a grizzly bear awakened from his hibernation. I preached the following Sunday as hard as I have ever preached on the subject of "Getting out of Spiritual Sinkholes." I described people who found themselves in spiritual sinkholes. Transportation, water, and power are cut off with no way out. I called the people out of those horrible sinkholes. I told them God wanted to reach down, heal their soul, lift them out of that miry clay, and set their feet on a rock. I declared the goodness of God in the midst of difficulties and tests. I proclaimed the greatness of God and His power that was sufficient to rescue us out of any of the enemy's snares. I called the people out of those pits of depression. I called them out of the sinkholes of discouragement and they came out, by the hundreds. They flooded the altars of our church, cried out to the Lord, and sought God's help, grace, comfort, and mercy. We rallied. The church grew up. We got stronger. Our faith recovered. What the Devil had meant for evil, God turned for good. What a great God we serve! What fabulous promises we have in His Word. We must refuse to stay in that hole of spiritual imprisonment. Instead, we must come out in Jesus' name! Paul and Silas refused to stay there. They sang and prayed until that Philippian prison was shaken by the presence of God and their chains fell off. Our chains will fall off too, if we will cry out to the Lord and call upon Him. He is mighty to deliver.

THE ENEMIES ARE REAL

Death is the last enemy to be destroyed, but even its destruction is imminent. The enemies of faith are real, but they can be defeated. The kingdoms of this world will become the kingdoms of our God. Every knee will bow and every tongue will confess that Jesus Christ is Lord, to the glory of God the Father. The enemies of sickness, hatred, bitterness, poverty, temptation, division, strife, fear, and lust all will be defeated and bow to the name of Jesus. Every disease must submit itself to the Name that is greater, higher, and above all names—the Name of Jesus Christ. Enemies that are real, tangible, and existent in this life will yield, be defeated, and eliminated from the life to come. In heaven there will be no more night, sickness, or fear, and every tear will be wiped away.

The power of the Holy Spirit is available to every believer now, in this life, to deal with these enemies. The Holy Ghost is the down payment of our promised inheritance. He is the divine deposit, the supernatural advance from God. He has been given to help us overcome and to enable us to live righteously and godly in this age. He is the Helper, the Comforter, and the Anointing. He will lead us into all truth. He will bring things to our remembrance. He will teach us and tutor us in the things of faith. He will empower us with the dunamis of God to overcome and defeat every enemy of faith in this world.

The apostle James tells us we should not be surprised when trials come against us to test our faith. We should rather count it all joy. Jesus said we were to rejoice and be exceedingly glad when we were persecuted for righteousness' sake. The testing of our faith will only create a stronger faith in us. We will grow from glory to glory and strength to strength, always progressing in our faith and possessing patience to mature. If we keep our eyes on Jesus and run our race with endurance, we will inherit the prize that He has planned for us. It is through faith and patience that we inherit the promises.

When the twelve spies returned from spying out the Promised Land under the ministry of Moses, ten of them returned with an evil report saying they were not able to possess the land. The giants are large, they exclaimed, and *"we were like grasshoppers...in their sight."*[1] Their bad report brought fear to the heart of the Hebrews. Unbelief and doubt will always bring fear of some kind.

Joshua and Caleb had a different spirit and they wholly followed after the Lord. As the only two who believed that they were able to go in and occupy the land, they challenged the people to believe God and go up at once to take possession of the land. They were not looking at the big enemies, they were looking at the bigger God! We know the enemies are big, in fact they are impossible to overcome by ourselves. But our God is bigger than our enemies, and He said that we could do all things through Him. This is the opposite of cowardly theology. This is Bible theology.

We should face our enemies and be strong in the Lord and in the power of His might. If our enemy is like a Goliath that looms in front of us with sword and spear, we can come against him in the name of the Lord. Our faith helps us confidently put our trust in a huge God who can handle any obstacle.

ATTACK ON THE POWER WORDS

If we were the Devil, which doctrines of the Bible would we attack? The Devil has tried to steal or spoil all the power words. Any Bible word that has a doctrine of power or authority associated with it has been an age-old target of the evil one. The enemy has tried to rob the Body of Christ of her rightful position and authority by attacking these words of influence, dominance, control, and supremacy. These are the muscle words of the kingdom of God:

+ Power—the *dunamis* of God's kingdom.

- ◆ Harvest—the worldwide reaping of souls into heaven.
- ◆ Holy Spirit—the agent of God's power on the earth today.
- ◆ Prosperity—the resources for the last day harvest.
- ◆ Healing—the strength of God for the bodies of the saints.
- ◆ Miracles—the validation of the Word of God by suspending natural law.
- ◆ Tongues—the beautiful languages of intercession.
- ◆ Authority—the enforcement of the kingdom of God.
- ◆ Discipleship—the process of building the Church.
- ◆ Deliverance—the inner freedom from all oppression.
- ◆ Holiness—the heart purity necessary for reigning.
- ◆ Charisma—the energy of the Spirit for service.
- ◆ Revival—the passionate desire of every true believer.
- ◆ Joy—the sweet strength of the people of God.
- ◆ Faith—the single key to everything in the kingdom of God.

In every case, there have been extremists and critics of all these words. Rather than dismissing them as too controversial, let us search the Word of God afresh and discover renewed faith in His Words.

The Devil hates the anointing, authority, the Word, and true believers. He will use any tactic to hinder the work of God and the faith of God's people. He will lie, cheat, murder, break the rules, and defy God. He is a blasphemer and a thief and will stop at nothing to prevent people from walking in faith. One brother said, "He will steal your lunch and then say God did it." We cannot listen to him. May we have a newly-tuned ear to the voice of God and pay attention to His words. That is where faith abides.

THE SHIELD OF FAITH

The Devil is the father of lies. He has been a liar from the beginning. He always attacks the Word of God. His favorite question is "Has God said?" He lies against the truth. He rails against any sound judgment. His age-old tactic is to malign the words of the One who is truth. He ridicules faith. Faith comes by hearing the Word of God. The Devil will do anything he can to keep people from hearing the words of truth, lest they believe, because all things are possible to the person who believes.

The Word of God is our sword against that Devil. Our belt is truth. Our shoes are Good News. Our helmet is salvation and our bulletproof vest is righteousness. Above all, our shield is faith. It quenches every fiery dart the wicked one launches. We can defeat him. Remember, we believe in a great big God and a little bitty devil.

The shield of faith quenches every fiery dart. We can extinguish, suppress, and stifle these flaming arrows of evil. The Greek language defines these darts as missiles, arrows, or javelins. It also tells us that these fiery weapons are expressions of the Devil's anger toward us. He is incensed and indignant. Through faith we can quench, extinguish, and stop these burning javelins from affecting others and us. As we expose some of these demonic arrows, let us determine, in faith, to resist the Devil and his schemes and stand fast in the power of the Lord. Here are some darts we should watch out for:

1. The dart of discouragement—everybody has times of discouragement. Abraham Lincoln said, "Let no feeling of discouragement prey upon you and in the end you are sure to succeed." We need to quench that arrow and be encouraged. The Lord God is with us.
2. The dart of weariness—the Devil will try to wear down the saints. Even Jesus took His disciples aside for times of rest during days of hectic ministry. We should get enough sleep, eat right, exercise, fellowship with good friends, and spend quality time with our family.
3. The dart of affliction—weakness, sickness, and affliction in our physical bodies is an attack of the Devil. But we can resist him. We need to rediscover the healing Scriptures and stand fast on the ground of the atonement and what Jesus did for us on the Cross. He took our sickness. By His stripes we were healed.
4. The dart of temptation—temptation is not sin. Yielding is. As we resist the Devil, he will flee. No temptation has come upon us that is not also common to others, but God always provides a way of escape. We can overcome. We must use the Word, use the blood of Jesus and douse that dart.
5. The dart of distraction—the Devil will use any number of good things to distract us from the Author and Finisher of our faith. We must not let a good thing, a good time, or good people rob us of

God's best. We can do that by staying focused on the Word of God and maintaining the fundamentals.

6. The dart of worldliness—like Lot, we are often vexed day and night with the filth of the world around us and must guard our eyes and hearts from its polluting influence. To love the world means the love of the Father is not in us. To become a friend of the world makes us an enemy of God.

THE VALLEY OF THE SHADOW

The valley of the shadow is often where we begin to doubt. Life circumstances can easily cast shadows on our faith. Circumstances like the death of a loved one, the tragedy of a life situation, a financial reversal, the falling of a trusted minister, the demise of a beloved church, or the death of an afflicted friend for whom we had fervently prayed. All of these things can take us into the land of darkness, into the place where doubt casts long shadows across God's Word and we begin to question God. It is here that faith is tested and confidence in God is proven.

In the valley of the shadow is where things are not as clear—light and darkness mix, faith and unbelief battle. It is here where His face is obscured in dimness. It is in this terrible valley that our faith is shaken to its core and we come face to face with our frailty. Our faith is not in our strength, it is in His. We must cheer up, look up, and not back up. He is working for us and already has a plan for our rescue. *"I will fear no evil."*[2] Faith is not trusting that we can get ourselves through this valley; faith believes that He can get us through. It is not self-confidence that enables us to navigate deep waters, but faith in the Lord of the wind and the waves. *"O you of little faith, why did you doubt?"*[3] This is precisely when God will meet and rescue us if we will turn to Him with all our heart. His rod and staff will comfort us. He will prepare a feast for us in the presence of our enemies and anoint us with fresh oil.

THE GREATEST ENEMIES OF FAITH

After a dynamic Sunday evening evangelistic event, we were having a time of prayer around the altar. Over one hundred people had come forward to receive Christ and were being ministered to by a large team of altar workers. Music was playing and people were weeping in repentance while others were laughing and rejoicing as they discovered freedom in Christ. Lives were being changed. I was overseeing the meeting and watching the proceedings with joy.

A young college student and his four female friends, all from a nearby Christian school, approached me and inquired if they could ask me a question. I soon realized that this young man's motive was not sincere. His intention was to look bold and intelligent in order to impress his peers. He sarcastically questioned, "We have been watching you and wondering why you are not praying with people. Do you feel you are too important?" I laughed, thinking he was joking, then tried to explain that we had trained a team of young workers for this particular event and I was overseeing the altar time to ensure everything ran smoothly. A novice critic, he continued to accuse me. As the discussion intensified, I recognized that I was being set up to prove a point. I finally asked him, "How old are you?" He retorted, "Twenty." I countered, "You are not old enough to talk to me like this." He finally crossed the line of propriety by attempting to touch me to enforce his point. Our faithful ushers stepped in and escorted him out of our building.

I was bothered by his accusations. I wondered, "Was I unconsciously projecting that attitude?" Upon further reflection, my only guilt was overreaction and defensive anger toward this foolish young man who was wrongly judging my motives and speaking evil of someone in authority. After the incident, I asked the Lord, "Why did this happen on such an otherwise glorious Sunday?" It was an easy answer for God. He was giving me a first-hand opportunity to encounter the greatest enemy of faith–legalistic religion.

The only people Jesus got angry with were religious people who judged Him and spoke evil of the things of God. His example made them look bad. The unbelieving retaliated against Him with legalistic zeal to prove their doctrine by demeaning His. Jesus loved sinners. He forgave prostitutes. He had dinner with Pharisees and tax collectors. He had no problem with the publicans. He was never angry with someone because of his or her sin. He was only grieved and indignant with hypocrites–bigoted zealots who honored their traditions above the Word of God. He would not tolerate self-righteous people who, out of spiritual pride, reacted to His righteous deeds.

Jesus warned His disciples to beware of the leaven of the Sadducees and Pharisees; that leaven of hypocrisy that spreads through the whole loaf until all is affected. A hypocritical spirit is spiritual pride and hardness of heart that results from constant resistance to truth. After a long time of hearing the Word and rationalizing it, a subtle deception will infect a person until he thinks the delusion is truth. How is this possible in church and among believers? It happens because people are *"hearers only"*[4] and because knowledge alone *"puffs up,"*[5] producing pride and the traditions of men that make the Word of God of no effect. If a person who calls himself a believer refuses to obey God's commands, he must rationalize his behavior in order to handle the inner conflict. That process of rationalization becomes deception and is usually defended vehemently against assaults of truth. People who operate in faith become a threat to people who do not. Fruitless pretenders will accost people who are producing the fruit of faith. The apostle Jude called them trees without fruit, clouds without water, and foaming waves of the sea.

Christians who stop growing in grace and knowledge of our Lord and Savior tend to misinterpret Scripture in light of their limited knowledge or past experience. No longer seeking God and searching His Word by meditating in it day and night, they stop growing spiritually. Unrepentant carnal habits begin to decrease their passion for Jesus and they easily backslide. Anyone who is passionate becomes a threat and is resisted, perhaps even persecuted. We can expect to be persecuted for righteousness' sake. Not everyone will appreciate our love for the Lord and zeal to obey Him.

One of the most amazing stories of the Gospels is Jesus' visit to His hometown of Nazareth. That Jesus Christ, the Son of God in person, could do no mighty work in that city is an atrocious testimony to their unbelief. They thought they knew Him, perceiving with only their natural understanding. They had no faith. Not only could He do no miracles, except for healing a few sick folks, but they also tried to kill Him. Their foolish unbelief hindered the effort of almighty God. Unbelief resists the plan of God and attempts to destroy it. We should not be surprised if people who call themselves believers resist us as we begin to grow in faith. Jesus told us to rejoice if that happens because that is how they treated the prophets of old. Unbelieving believers will always attempt to pull true believers down to their level of making God small and defining Him based on the traditions of men. As the Psalms described them, they have limited the Holy One of Israel.

God will set a banqueting table for us in the presence of our enemies. We should not fear for He will be with us and comfort us as we discern and defeat these enemies of faith. As we describe how the Devil uses people to try and halt our faith, we cannot make the mistake of thinking our enemy is human. *"We do not wrestle against flesh and blood, but against principalities, against powers, against the rulers of the darkness of this age, against spiritual hosts of wickedness in the heavenly places."* [6] Our enemy is still the same invisible and demonic Devil, the Dragon, that serpent of old, the accuser of the brethren, Satan.

THIRTEEN MARKS OF SPIRITUAL PRIDE

Spiritual pride and hypocrisy is an appalling spirit. It is the spirit that crucified our Lord. It opposed the work of the apostles. It hindered the planting of churches, and it still combats true believers today.

Solomon received revelation of the things that God hates. Seven things are listed as an abomination to God. Among them are a proud look, a lying tongue, and one who sows discord among brethren. God hates this attitude. Jesus rose up against people that made public displays of religion but inwardly were like tombs full of bones.

Spiritual pride will make itself known. Like a peacock, it will unfold its feathers and display a temper of arrogance that will give it away. Those who are bound by this attitude have some common characteristics:

1. Exclusive Revelation—they believe they have insight from God that others do not
2. Superiority—they believe themselves to be better than others
3. Unbelief—they refuse to exercise genuine faith or trust the Lord
4. Judgment—they are critical and judge the motives of others
5. Debate—they make a man an offender for a word or semantics

6. Conceit—they think of themselves more highly than they should
7. Ambition—they promote themselves
8. Manipulation—they attempt to control others emotionally
9. Strife—they debate and dispute over words
10. Prejudice—they are a respecter of persons with a spirit of bigotry
11. Offense—they react with bitterness and unforgiveness
12. Ignorance—they err in judgment because of a deliberate lack of knowledge
13. Hypocrisy—they hide sin in their own hearts

If we have any of these characteristics visible in our lives, spiritual pride is knocking at our door. We need to repent of these characteristics and strive to remain humble in our spirituality.

NO ONE REMEMBERS CRITICS

Few of us can name all twelve spies who were sent by Moses to spy out the land of Canaan. However, we no doubt recall Joshua and Caleb. The names of the other ten who came back with an evil report, however, have lapsed into oblivion. They had a spirit of unbelief. They rejected God. They rebelled against Moses. They opened a door to the spirit of fear. They wavered and died under the judgment of God. Outside of being listed as spies, they are forgotten.

My friend, Dr. Michael Brown, of note as both an author and teacher at the Brownsville revival in Pensacola, Florida, was ministering in our church and quoted a list of people's names. "Do you recognize any of these names?" he asked. He went on to explain that they were the unremembered critics of great revivalists including John Wesley, Jonathan Edwards, and Charles Finney. The latter are remembered as great men of faith, but their critics have passed into nonexistence.

Our Lord described His opponents as uprooted plants and blind leaders of the blind. He said if the blind lead the blind, they will both fall into the ditch. He told His disciples to *"leave them alone."*[7] To continue to grow in faith, move on in God, and do His perfect will. We must learn to ignore the critics and stay the course. There will always be those who do not agree with us and ridicule or resist our faith. Even well-meaning souls, family members, and friends may try to dishearten or hinder us. Our foundation is the Word of God. We must build on it. With graciousness and determination, we must learn to dismiss their words and carry on with that *rhema*-word we received from the Lord.

VICTORY OVER THE DEVIL

No weapon formed against me will prosper, but every tongue that rises against me in judgment I will condemn. This is the heritage of the servants of the Lord and my righteousness in God. Greater is He that is in me than he that is in the world. The Lord will arise and my enemies will be scattered. When the Devil comes against me one way, he will flee seven different directions. And when the enemy comes in like a flood, the Spirit of the Lord will lift up a standard against him. The Lord scatters all evil with His eyes. The God of peace will soon crush Satan underneath my feet.

I will resist the Devil and he will flee. I will resist him firm in my faith. I will put on the whole armor of God and stand against the wiles of the Devil. I will not wrestle flesh and blood, but principalities and powers and rulers of the darkness of this age, against spiritual hosts of wickedness in heavenly places. I will be strong in the Lord and in the power of His might. I will be able to withstand in the evil day and having done all, stand. The Devil, like a roaring lion, goes about seeking whom he may devour, but I will resist him firm in my faith, knowing that the same sufferings are required of my brethren who are in the world.

MY HELP IN TROUBLE

God is our Helper, our Hiding Place and Shield. He is Jehovah Gmolah— the God of Recompense; Jehovah Makkeh—the Lord who strikes our enemies; Jehovah Nissi—the Lord our Banner; Jehovah Sabbaoth—the Lord of Hosts; Jehovah Shalom—the Lord our Peace. He is the Just Judge, the Keeper, the Lord mighty in battle, the Lord of Lords, the Lord of Peace and the Lord who makes a way in the sea.

He is our Master, the Mighty One, and our Fortress. He is my Glory and the Lifter of my head, my Safe Refuge, the One who becomes a Shield for me. He is the Power of God, my Rock and Rod. He is the Shade at my right hand, my Shepherd, the Strength of my heart, my Stronghold, a Sun and Shield, a very present help in trouble.

With the Heart Man Believes

My soul doth magnify the Lord, and my spirit hath rejoiced in God my Saviour.
Luke 1:46-47 (KJV)

The number one killer of adults in our nation is heart disease. Perhaps this natural problem is a sign of a greater spiritual problem. Sin in the heart can destroy a person and condemn them to an eternity of separation from God. One of the most insidious evils in the heart of man is the disease of unbelief, infecting even people who call themselves "believers." If a Christian ceases to exercise faith and tolerates the spirit of unbelief, the hardening of the heart will eventually lead to sin.

The Scriptures are filled with references to the heart because the Bible is a heart book. God is after our hearts. The New Covenant established by Jesus is a covenant of the heart. Jesus' teachings always dealt with the human heart and not just externals. *"Out of the abundance of the heart the mouth speaks"*[1] and life flows. We are admonished to guard our heart with all diligence because out of it flow all the issues of life.

The heart is our faith hardware or the center of our faith system. Paul tells the Romans it is with the heart that man believes. We are saved when we believe with all our heart. King David said he had hidden God's Word in his heart so that he would not sin. He prayed that the meditation of his heart would be acceptable to God. He also fixed his heart to sing God's praise. It is the heart that the Lord examines when He tests men's souls. *"As [a man] thinks in his heart, so is he."*[2] It is out of the abundance of the heart that a person's mouth speaks, and it is the good and honest heart that becomes the rich soil in which the seed of the kingdom takes root and brings forth fruit. It is with the heart that a person believes.

We do not believe with our heads. Faith does not operate out of the human mind. The mind is the realm of the soul and relates to the five senses of the human body, whereas the heart is the realm of the spirit and is wired to operate in faith, the spiritual terrain of the things of God. Faith is a spiritual exercise. We are admonished in the Bible to *"trust in the Lord with all [our] heart"* and not lean *"on [our] own understanding."*[3] The carnal mind, at enmity with God, must be renewed in order to do the will of God. Paul tells the Romans to be *"transformed by the renewing"* of their minds.[4] He tells the Ephesians to *"be renewed in the spirit of [their] mind."*[5] Our thoughts are not naturally God's thoughts; therefore, we must meditate on God's Word day and night if we want good success. Every day we need the mind of Christ to know what He thinks about our decisions, choices, desires, goals, and relationships. We need to learn to think like Him, but thinking is not necessarily believing. The renewing of our mind is the process of ensuring that our mind maintains pace with our spirit. Many times, in the pathway of faith, we will be challenged to bypass our natural thinking and operate in supernatural believing. This is the nature of faith working in the heart of man.

When the apostle Paul reasoned with philosophers at the Areopagus in Athens, in Acts chapter seventeen, he preached the message of the Gospel in the language of philosophy as he described to them the unknown god. He preached a heart message to people dominated by head thinking. They squandered their time in discussion of human philosophies. Paul described them as very religious and yet ignorant of the living God. They were lovers of wisdom, which is the meaning of the Greek word for philosophy. But the wisdom they loved was the wisdom of men, not the wisdom of God. They loved the sound of new words and new theories. They loved to debate concepts but they did not have a love of the truth. Their *"foolish hearts were dark-*

ened[6] as the book of Romans describes. They were not heart people searching for truth. They were religious critics. Today, some churches are filled with Christians who do the same by attempting to reason their way through the kingdom. The kingdom of God is a kingdom of faith and faith happens in the heart.

As the primary believing mechanism, the heart must be guarded from faith-destroying sources. Anti-faith viruses will attempt to attack our operating systems and ruin our ability to function in God's kingdom. Solomon warned us to *"keep [our] heart with all diligence for out of it spring all the issues of life."*[7] Paul told the Philippians to make their requests known to God with thanksgiving and then the *"peace of God...will guard your hearts and minds."*[8] If our heart is damaged it will hinder our ability to believe.

Behind our house, on a golf course, are two marshy ponds that abound with mosquitoes, bugs, and dragonflies. In the early summer, the frogs begin their seasonal serenade and multiplication process. The grounds crew must regularly clean the ponds making sure they stay fresh and clear of contaminating sources. A hurting heart, the breeding ground for unbelief, is like those ponds grown stagnate. Our hearts were meant to flow with living water like cascading streams—bringing life to all who pass by. Stopping the flow and clogging the drain multiplies the critters of unbelief, worry, fear, and bitterness. It will pollute the riverbed of our heart, resulting in a diminished flow of faith. We must keep the waters of faith flowing through a pure and uncontaminated heart. Following is a list of the heart conditions that we need to avoid in order to keep our hearts pure.

A WOUNDED HEART

Our church has become a place of refuge for many battle-worn spiritual soldiers and a safe house for those fleeing from their enemies. It is inevitable that offenses will come, but church should be a place of peace and a haven of safety. Solomon said that the spirit of a man will sustain him in time of weakness; but if his spirit is wounded, what can he bear? A wounded heart will handicap our faith and limit our potential. Jesus' heart bled for us so that the bleeding of our wounded hearts could be stopped. The Lord can stop our issue of blood, like the woman of the Gospels, if we will reach out in faith and touch His garment. We must believe to be healed of our wounds.

A POISONED HEART

A former pastor once cautioned me, "Don't let them hurt you." He had given up on his church, his ministry and livelihood, and later his marriage. He was warning me, out of legitimate pain, to beware of cruel people. There is, however, only one way to escape from hurtful people —go to heaven! As long as we are in this life, there will be offenses and hurts. The goal should not be to look for ways of escape, but rather to guard and protect our hearts through love and forgiveness.

I have seen many offended believers, poisoned by bitterness and unforgiveness, self-destruct from the inside out. They permitted an unchecked demolition of their faith until all infrastructure of character was weakened and their life collapsed. It destroyed them and injured those they loved. The apostle Paul admonishes us to be tenderhearted; forgiving one another as God, for Christ's sake, forgave us. Forgiveness, like a key, unlocks the prison cells of those we have incarcerated through our bitterness. Our own deliverance from the bondage of bitterness is determined by their deliverance. If we will release others from revenge, faith will flow again.

A POLLUTED HEART

Impurity kills. If we suppose we can open our heart to perversion and unbridled lust without consequences, we are deceived and embracing a delusion. We will taint, poison, and corrode our faith, masking our true emotions and warping our perceptions. Lust wars against the soul, Peter warned. Spiritually, we will fall into a fog bank of confusion, knowing truth but approving lies and flirting with evil. Our weakened will can be renewed and strengthened only through a time of repentance, confession, cleansing, and trusting in the sanctifying power of the blood of Jesus. The only remedy is to put our faith and trust in Him and in His power to set us free from fleshly bondage.

A STOLEN HEART

A cold or lukewarm relationship with the Lover of our soul is a symptom of idolatry. Another lover has stolen our hearts. Stolen waters may initially be sweet, but they will turn bitter in the stomach and eventually harden our spiritual arteries. If we allow ourselves to be enticed by another god and bow down to its charm or domination, our faith will be weakened like Samson with a haircut. Idolatry is a violation of fundamental faith. It is turning from the One who can save, heal, and forgive, to the gods that have no power except to enslave.

A HARDENED HEART

A hard heart is the consequence of believing a lie. Wearied in well doing, tired in the fight of faith, the heart hardens, as Hebrews describes it, *"through the deceitfulness of sin."*[9] Faith is rejected and the heart caves, crashes, and quits the battle. No longer believing, we become purposely cynical—jesting about things sacred, making light of things divine, and mocking what once stirred our hearts in spiritual passion.

A spouse blames God because his mate has rejected him for another. An offended church member walks away from the church, rejecting faith. A young man cannot seem to get free from a dominating habit. The human tendency is to give up, give in, and capitulate. Faith can grow again, break up the fallow ground of our hearts, and soften the soil of our spirits with the rain of His presence. We must not give up! The Lord can help us.

A PROUD HEART

When faith is working, pride is lurking. Prayers are being answered. Sicknesses are being healed. Mountains are moving and financial needs are being met with a surplus. It might seem that all is well when faith is functioning. But if a believer is operating outside the parameters of God's character and nature, his exploits may be counter-productive.

If faith is associated with external achievement like clothing, jewelry, or technology toys, then it is being prostituted. Faith was meant to be used for the extension of God's kingdom and the fulfillment of His purpose, not for carnal exhibit or show and certainly not for selfish gain. Moses warned the people not to allow their heart to be lifted up in a time of prosperity and forget God.

One of the most vulnerable attitudes is that of a proud heart. Mountain-moving faith without love is pointless. Faith for the impossible without compassion for the probable amounts to the gullible. Samson did not know the Lord departed from him and presumed to go out, as at other times, and win the battle, but he found that his own strength and skill was not sufficient. Neither is ours. As Scripture points out, we need to humble ourselves under the mighty hand of God and keep putting our trust in a faithful Creator.

SNARES TO OUR OWN FAITH

Each of us has received a measure of faith and is expected to be a good steward of it. In protecting this precious and priceless gift, beware of these six snares:

1. Fear of man—if we are more concerned about what people think than what God thinks, we will be bound by the fear of man and incapable of sincere faith in God.
2. Reactionary theology—overreaction to an extreme in doctrine will only perpetuate the opposite extreme and further polarize people from the truth. We cannot formulate principles or build any area of our lives on reactionary theology. It is like shifting sand and very precarious.
3. Being wise in our own opinions—any private interpretation of the Scriptures is treacherous. Faith is not trusting in our opinion, but rather trusting in God's opinion, His word. In the journey of our faith, we are always growing. We will never have the full revelation of God's Word and what it means; there is always more for us to learn and discover. Humility will keep us teachable, maturing, and growing in the grace of God.
4. Analytical reasoning—trusting in our own understanding and reasoning will divert us from the track of faith and into the realm of mere logic. Belief occurs in the heart, not in the head.

5. Personal insecurity—personal insecurity can prejudice our interpretation of the truth of God's Word and consequently distort our faith. Being unsure of our own spiritual parameters is an indication of our need to grow in knowledge of Him. It also is not a wise premise on which to defend our personal opinions.

6. Biblical ignorance—ignorance of the Word can lead to spiritual captivity and destruction. This necessitates the believer's continued growth in the knowledge of God through the daily reading and meditating of the Scriptures.

INCREASING OUR SHIELD

In ancient battles, the shield was the primary defensive weapon. It was readied and prepared for battle with fresh oil to deflect the arrows and blows of the enemy. Similarly, our shield of faith should be freshly anointed and prepared for our protection. Here are four keys to enhancing the protection of our shields:

1. The Bible says knowledge increases strength. We need to become a dedicated student of the Bible and enlarge our faith resources.

2. The fellowship of the "faith-filled" is our natural habitat. We should attend church regularly, committing ourselves to a "faith-filled" congregation that will edify and provoke us toward love and good works.

3. We must learn to fight the good fight of faith. Paul described it as a fight of faith, for which we must prepare, stir ourselves, get a little indignant, and battle. We cannot just give in to the enemy, but must resist, fight back, and win the victory.

4. We should always speak the Word of God to our situation. With it we can take aim and fire. We should fill our hearts with Scripture and out of that abundance let our mouths speak. Stockpiled ammunition of faith provides the Holy Spirit with a vast spiritual arsenal to instantly quicken that *rhema*-word to our hearts. The Word of God breeds faith in a believer's heart. Praise and thanksgiving are evidence of that faith and miracles are spawned by it.

DO NOT DRAW BACK

When our faith is under attack, we may find ourselves assaulted by a spirit of heaviness and discouragement. To ensure a quick and decisive triumph over these skirmishes, we must devise a pre-battle plan like a coach who studies his opponent to prepare pre-game strategies for winning. We should determine a course of action to rescue ourselves from the enemies of faith, using the secret weapons found in Scripture.

The collection of verses that directly precedes the great faith chapter of the Bible, chapter ten of the book of Hebrews, provides some great ammunition for attacks on our faith. We are reminded not to cast away our confidence because, after having done the will of God, we need endurance to receive the promise. The timetable may seem unending to us, but He who promised to help us is on His way.

Drawing back is not an option. The Bible warns against going back to "Egypt" as the children of Israel wanted to do in the wilderness. We are not to *"turn back"*[10] like the children of Ephraim did in the day of battle. Jesus warned us to remember Lot's wife and not look back. Paul exhorted the Philippians to forget the things that are behind, reach toward the things that are ahead, and press toward the goal. Hebrews teaches us if anyone draws back, God will take no pleasure in him.

The disciples all forsook Jesus in His hour of crisis. Others who had followed Him drew back because they could not handle His teachings. Demas forsook the apostle Paul for the present world. The Bible tells us that it would be better for some not to have known the way of righteousness than to turn from it. Hebrews tells us that, in some cases, it is impossible to renew individuals to repentance if they fall away. Drawing back is sin. The Bible says it clearly, *"whatever is not from faith is sin."*[11] We have to fight the fight of faith, shake ourselves, and get stirred up. We are not those who draw back, but those who believe—and it delivers our soul. Our mind, will, and emotions are preserved when we act in faith and take authority over our own soul.

Retreat should never be an alternative. God is always advancing and He expects us to do the same. Faith is never backward, it is always moving forward. It is advancing, going ahead, marching into, stepping out, and reaching for those things that are ahead.

THE SPIRIT OF UNBELIEF

The spirit of unbelief is a dreadful spiritual and emotional bondage that ensnares its victims, some of whom never recover from the devastation. Opening ourselves to this enslaving attitude will entangle us with chains of skepticism, suspicion, and pride. It will color our perceptions like a person wearing green lenses—everything they see is green. When we live like this, we cannot see faith anywhere. Our countenance sours. Our words become caustic, and no one enjoys being around us unless it is someone equally as miserable.

These people often form small groups that break from churches, cutting themselves off from their only hope. They are like Jonah and run from the call of God, neglecting their own mercy and alienating themselves from their source of rescue. They are like the prodigal son on a wild spending spree of carnality, alienated from the father's love. In sincerity, they feel it their responsibility to burst what they believe are bubbles of false hope in others.

Faith is an unbeliever's only hope or lifeline in the storm. It is the answer for people who need healing, help, wisdom, provision, forgiveness, and deliverance from confusion and disillusionment. I have often witnessed unbelieving people call on believers for assistance in a time of crisis and depleted options. As a last ditch effort, they call for people of faith in hopes of gaining some supernatural means that will solve an impossible situation like curing a terminal disease, saving a wayward child, rescuing an impending bankruptcy, or restoring a wounded marriage.

Faith pleases God, and He is looking for those with hearts of hope who are living the life of faith. Those who sow the seeds of faith have the hope of harvest even when the storm is brewing, the enemy is knocking, the disease is devouring, and the Devil is roaring.

We must return to the simplicity of God's Word and repent from a heart of unbelief, which the writer to the Hebrews calls evil. We should turn our back on skepticism and doubting and get back on the solid ground of faith, firmly founded on the unerring and infallible Word of the living God—the Bible.

WHAT TO DO WHEN FAITH DOES NOT SEEM TO WORK

We were doing our best to walk by faith but the situation was not resolved the way we had envisioned it. Why didn't God let us purchase the K-Mart building for our growing church? Why didn't it work out as we had planned? We had prayed in faith and asked according to what we believed to be His will.

We do not always see the whole picture. The Bible says we see in part. Our responsibility is to speak to our mountain, ask largely, believe God, confess at the level of our faith, and then trust. The Lord knows us, our situation, and our needs better than we do. He is such a good Father, answering our prayers as His will dictates, in spite of our immature requests and shortsighted vision. The answer comes, but not always like we thought it would. God always gives us better than what we ask for. The Lord had so dramatically and prophetically led us to that first location in Bellevue that unless God closed the doors and obviously spoke to me again I did not want to move. Many prayers had been focused on acquiring the K-Mart building, and we were still looking for our "blue light special" miracle from God!

I called for a day of prayer and fasting to seek God's direction for our future. Doors had begun to close. The K-Mart organization renewed their lease on their building. The city denied our request for a conditional use permit to expand our church, and then the landlord gave us sixty days to move. As these three huge doors closed within days of one another, the Holy Spirit began to reveal His plan. I recalled a prophecy by David Schoch a year before, given during a Wednesday night service as he was addressing our church. In the middle, he interrupted his sermon to prophesy, "Get ready. Change is coming. But it's not going to come the way you think and it's not going to come the way you want. But it will come and you'll have to make your mind up, 'Will we go with God?'"

It was time for change and this time the change was huge. We had focused all our prayers and faith on that building and property and now the doors were all closed. I suppose the Lord knew what it would take for me to move. I had been so determined to stay and possess that land, that I had not considered the possibility that we might have to cross some other Jordan and occupy some other territory. Still wanting to hear a word from God, I received three words very quickly. The first came that Saturday morning after the landlord had given us the sixty-day ultimatum. I was so angry with the owner of the building I almost missed hearing the voice of God. The Lord spoke crystal clear into my spirit that morning as I sat among the men for our prayer breakfast, "You can go now." It had been a long time since I had felt that released. I was so happy.

The second word came that next Wednesday. Bishop Joseph Garlington of Pittsburgh was our guest speaker for the weekend of our fifth anniversary celebration. He preached from Deuteronomy about the children of Israel circling their mountain long enough and God telling them to turn north. This new building we were considering was six miles to the north and we were certainly tired of circling the mountain of resistance with our landlord.

Again, providentially, David Schoch was the other scheduled speaker for the week. It was just over one year from the time of his word to us about "doors of change." During the Thursday morning service of our anniversary celebration he shared a simple thought, saying "I believe the Lord is going to do a miracle in this church in seven days." That afternoon, I confided in Brother Schoch and Bishop Garlington, informing them of our dilemma. I had told them earlier that we were looking at another building, but I had not given them any details. I coveted their counsel and prayers in what was possibly the most important move we had ever made. I expressed my concern about leaving and creating any confusion with the people, since I had made such a big deal about staying and believing for this land. I also inquired as to what they thought about the past prophecies and how the Lord had so sovereignly led us to this location. David settled the questions of my heart with one simple statement. "Prophecies are not forever and the prophetic word didn't say you would stay here indefinitely. Go." And go we did. In fact, it was seven days exactly from the day we received notice to vacate our rental space until the signing of the lease papers on the new building. When we made the announcement on Saturday night, our people not only celebrated, they also felt a sense of relief. God had honored our faith, led us clearly for five years, and was now honoring us with something better than what we had asked for.

When our faith seems to take a left turn, right turn, or U-turn, we need to just look around and know it is probably God leading us toward the answer to our prayers. We need to remember that Abraham did not know where he was going, but went in faith. We might not know our location or direction, but we should be at peace because we are following the One who never gets lost. He is the Way! We should follow Him with all our heart.

EVERYTHING WORKS FOR GOOD

Nothing can separate me from the love of God. All things will work together for good for me because I love God and am part of the called according to His purpose. Even what the Devil means for evil, God will turn for good. I am more than a conqueror through Him who loved me. And I am giving thanks in everything, for this is the will of God in Christ Jesus for me.

The battle is not mine but the Lord's. He is the One who fights my battles for me and defends me against my enemies. He is the God who strikes my enemies. He is my Rock and Refuge. He lifts up my head against my enemies. He is the Lord mighty in battle. My enemies will come against me one way but they will flee seven different directions. The Lord will arise and scatter His enemies.

HE IS THE LORD WHO FIGHTS FOR YOU

He is our Advocate, the Almighty, the Angel of the Lord, the Arm of the Lord, and the Captain of our salvation. He is the Defender and the Deliverer. He is El Roi—The One who sees, and El Shaddai—God Almighty. He is the Father of the fatherless and the Friend that sticks closer than a brother, the God of Mercy, the God of my life, the God of Peace, and the God of Truth. He is the God who performs all things for me, my Good Shepherd and Guide even to death.

CHAPTER NINE

The Prayer of Faith

Let all those who seek You rejoice and be glad in You;
And let those who love Your salvation say continually, "Let God be magnified!"
Psalm 70:4

Although I was a minister, I realized that I did not really know how to pray. But in 1986 I began a personal discovery into a realm of spiritual reality that forever altered my destiny. I had been in the ministry for thirteen years and an ordained elder for more than seven when I started to use the Lord's Prayer as a model for daily prayer. Once I began to pray regularly, consistently, and biblically, I realized that my prayer life prior to that time had been virtually non-existent. I prayed over meals, when in crisis, for my children when I put them to bed, and my wife and I would sometimes hold hands in bed and mumble a few words before falling asleep. As one of the pastors of our church I joined our congregation in corporate prayer before each service; but a daily, prolonged prayer life was new to me. I recognized I had knowledge of a doctrine but limited experience in prayer.

Like many believers, I embraced the name of Christ, attended church, owned a Bible, said "amen" to preaching and teaching, but did not practice what I was taught. I was not obedient to the Scriptures. I was not a doer of the Word in this vital area of my life. I was lacking and anemic in my spiritual life and relationship with the Lord—and I was a pastor. How many equally ignorant believers know about the truth but do not know the God of truth? How many who call them-selves believers are not exercising the faith to boldly and biblically make their requests known to God? How many good people are sitting in churches and hearing about prayer, faith, or the power of the Holy Spirit, but not practicing it? I am concerned for a large population of the Body of Christ who are hearers but not doers of the Word, fat with truth but out of shape in obedience, acting spiritual on Sundays but living fairly carnal the other six days of the week. How distant we can be while thinking we are close to God. How far we stray from the New Testament standard and example of true faith. How anemic our spiritu-al lives can be when we do not pray the prayer of faith on a daily basis. It must grieve God when His children whom He bore, do not bow their knees, close their closet doors, shut themselves away, and wait on Him for His counsel, help, and comfort. The wings of an eagle certainly await those who do.

When I was first given a daily prayer guide based on the Lord's Prayer, I was impressed with the simplicity and biblical basis. It provided a simple outline of the Prayer as a pattern for praying over an hour. I could not imagine praying for an entire sixty minutes—what would I pray about? As I reviewed the prayer card I thought to myself, *I can do this. I can learn to pray.* Using the plan every day I found my prayer life expanding from three or four minutes to more than twenty or thirty. Progressively, I learned to pray for more than an hour and marveled that I had not discovered the power of this grace earlier in my life and min-istry. I was amazed that there were so many fundamental issues to pray about and a little ashamed that I had neglected to do so. Now, years later, we have developed our own prayer guide based on that same revelation and do our best to teach these principles to our Seattle congregation.

Before coming to this revelation, I cannot recall one sermon on the how-to of prayer. Over the decades of growing up in church I had heard a lot of messages preached on prayer, but I had never heard any-one teach on how to pray. Studying how Jesus taught His disciples to pray through the Lord's Prayer, I realized He was giving them a model, outline, and guide for how to pray. Learning how to pray, especially praying in faith, is the key to seeing our faith become a reality and our dreams fulfilled.

When we launched our church in 1992, we prayed. We had to. We would not have survived without prayer and an understanding of how to get a hold of God. We prayed for wisdom. We prayed for direction. We prayed for the right location. We prayed for the name of the church. We prayed for finances. We prayed for people, leaders, and souls to be saved. We prayed for families and individuals to be added to our church. We prayed for miracles and the demonstration of the power of God. We prayed for divine help. We even prayed for good weather. (We live in Seattle.)

THE POWER OF PRAYER

Exactly why God requires prayer in order to accomplish His will is one of those heavenly mysteries that we may not fully comprehend this side of paradise. Prayer is an amazing and unusual force that employs the voices and faith of mortal men to move the hand of almighty God. Prayer reaches to the throne room of heaven and prints out petitions before the King of all kings. It is the supernatural communication vehicle of faith. It is the hotline to heaven. It is the original email, instant in its access to the divine hard drive. It is the language of humility, the song of sincerity, and the voice of the believer.

God has designed His kingdom in such a way that Christians must pray in order to mobilize the assistance of God on their behalf. John Wesley is credited with a quote that states, "God does nothing apart from the prayers of His people." Daily, the Lord awaits our petitions and supplications as we in similar fashion await His commands and directives. Prayer is the human-divine connection and communion of spirits that secures the will of God in the lives of finite people. Prayer is the act of the human will to petition divine assistance. It is the spiritual launching pad that sends anointed intercession-missiles into orbit around the throne of God. Prayer is the lover's language between the heavenly Groom and the earthly bride. Prayer is a primary act of faith.

People pray, God acts. Humans intercede, the Divine intervenes. Weak ones cry out, and the Mighty One responds. The infirm appeal to Him, and the Healer stretches out His hand. The poor humble themselves in His sight, the Provider lifts them up out of the ash heap. The pauper asks for aid, the Prince of Peace sends help from the sanctuary.

The widow is persistent in her requests, the Judge of all the earth answers her speedily. The sinner begs forgiveness, the Savior covers sin. Man calls, God answers. This is prayer.

We may not fully understand it, but we do know that God used the prayers of prophets, kings, peasants, and prisoners to accomplish impressive things throughout biblical history. Abraham prayed and interceded for the city of Sodom. Moses also used intercession to plead with God for the lives of His rebellious people. Moses became the symbol of intercession when he lifted his hands on the mountain as Joshua fought the battle in the valley. His hands eventually became so heavy that Aaron and Hur had to hold them up. As long as the hands of Moses were extended over the conflict, Joshua and the armies of Israel prevailed.

David must have had special communion with God to write the heart-searching, soul-wrenching collection of songs we call Psalms. Truly, he had the heartbeat of God, and the Lord loved him and listened to his prayers. As a boy in the fields, a captain with Saul, a fugitive, and then a king himself, David was the man with the God-shaped heart. When his son Solomon reigned in his stead, God showed His divine approval of the sacrifices surrounding the dedication of the Temple. He came down in the fire and the cloud, and declared that He would listen to prayers made in that place and keep His eyes open to watch over the nation.

Nehemiah led God's people in prayers that preserved the rebuilding of Jerusalem, as did the scribe Ezra. Others were also fervent and strong in their prayers to God. Daniel, Esther, Job, King Jehoshaphat, Hezekiah, Isaiah, Jeremiah—all employed the clout of prayer. Many of the kings, queens, prophets, and people of the Old Testament knew the power of prayer.

The New Testament opens with Zacharias entering the Holy place to offer incense and prayers for the people and being interrupted by the angel Gabriel. The New Covenant testimony concludes with John being in the Spirit on the Lord's day and seeing visions of things to come. In between is the record of the early church that modeled prayer more than any single group in biblical history.

After Jesus left the earth, the first disciples and apostles manifested their passion for constant and corporate persistence in prayer. They were praying on the day of Pentecost in the Upper Room when the Holy Spirit fell. They continued steadfastly in prayers after Pentecost. Peter and John performed one of the first miracles on the lame man as they went up to the Temple at the hour of prayer. An angel visited Cornelius as he prayed, and Peter fell into a trance as he prayed. These two visions opened the door of the Gospel to the Gentiles. The church prayed around the clock for Peter while he was in prison and was surprised when he appeared at their door, having left jail in the middle of the night with the help of an angelic visitor. Paul and Silas pioneered a church at Philippi, meeting with some women at the river where prayer was customarily made. Later, after being imprisoned for delivering a slave girl from a demon, they were liberated from prison by an earthquake as they prayed and sang at the midnight hour. The first generation Church demonstrated what a church is supposed to look like—people of prayer who prayed with great faith.

The apostle Paul, author of much of the New Testament, was a man of serious prayer. He mentioned numerous times how he was praying for the churches, believers, other leaders, and his spiritual children. He wrote to them that he was praying in faith that they would grow, be given wisdom, and that Christ would be fully formed in them. He described prayer as spiritual warfare in need of a full suit of armor. He also asked his brethren to remember him in their prayers and to pray without ceasing for the work of God.

THE LORD'S PRAYER AS A PATTERN

Jesus Himself prayed. In the Gospels of Matthew, Mark, Luke, and John we see Jesus modeling the prayer life that the apostles would pattern as the Church was established. If the Son of God needed to pray while on earth, how much more all the sons of God? If He is the model and prototype and we are somewhere further down the assembly line, then we desperately need to pray.

Jesus told us to ask, seek, and knock. He said if we ask we will receive, if we knock it will be opened to us, and if we seek we will find. Everyone who asks, knocks, and seeks will receive. He told His disciples that they had asked nothing in His name up to that point and urged them to ask the Father in His name, that they might receive and their joy be full. He encouraged them to be like the widow before the unjust judge and persist until they received what they wanted. He taught them to enter their closet and pray to their Father in secret, and that whatever they asked for in secret would be given them openly.

The most dramatic revelation about prayer came after Jesus had been praying in the early morning hours and His disciples were looking for Him. They found Him, watched Him, and waited until He was finished praying. Then they made the inquiry that forever changed their lives: *"Lord, teach us to pray, as John also taught his disciples."*[1] The main Intercessor, who still lives and stands at the right hand of the Father interceding for you and me today, had come to them and for the first time in history demonstrated true and powerful prayer.

His response has become the classic description of prayer. More believers have repeated His response over the centuries than perhaps any other Scripture. It is the Prayer. It is the Model. It has been called the Lord's Prayer, although it might be better named the Disciple's Prayer. It is the heavenly revelation of how to pray. It is a collection of some seventy words that sets the standard for prayer and proper presentation to God. However, this prayer was never meant to be magic words. It was not intended to be a repetitive spiritual poem or some secret mantra to be chanted to the unknown God.

When Jesus taught His disciples to pray, He made that point clear in Matthew's gospel. Jesus' words are, *"In this manner...pray..."*[2] In Luke's gospel, Jesus says, *"When you pray, say..."* [3] Jesus did not intend them to quote Him or to repeat words. This is obvious since He admonished them not to be like the hypocrites who prayed on street corners to be seen by men, or to reiterate words like the heathen did in vain repetition. He anticipated, however, that they would follow this pattern, use this model, adhere to this outline, and employ this guide for daily prayer.

As found in Matthew chapter six, verses nine through thirteen, there are seven divisions of the Lord's Prayer. As I personally learned to pray, I discovered that these seven areas of daily supplication and petition helped me focus my faith in such a way that all the basics of my life were regularly covered in prayer.

"Our Father in heaven, hallowed be Your name"

This is how we enter His presence—with praise and thanksgiving. Each morning we come boldly by the blood of Jesus and approach the throne of grace to ask for His help. We come with thanksgiving, honoring and blessing His name for all He is and all He does. A time to worship Him, thank Him and minister to Him in praise should precede the presentation of any petitions.

"Your kingdom come"

This continues with, *"Your will be done on earth as it is in heaven."* This is our destiny and authority in Christ. We are agents of the King. We are His servants, and we are here to do His will. Every day we align our will to do His. We take up our cross, deny ourselves, and prepare to follow Him through the day. This is the point at which we petition Him for the primary issues we are facing and ask for His divine intervention.

"Give us this day our daily bread"

This is the prayer-point of provision when we ask for our needs to be met in a tangible, material way so that we can then focus on blessing others and fulfilling the commission we have been given.

"And forgive us our debts, as we forgive our debtors"

Rare is the day that does not include some kind of offense from another. This prayer-point addresses relational issues by daily preparing our heart to stay tender and ready to forgive.

"And do not lead us into temptation, but deliver us from the evil one"

At this point, we engage in spiritual warfare and prepare ourselves for a day of conquest. Our adversary, the Devil, is seeking to devour us; so we must put on the whole armor of God, resist him, and be ready to walk in victory.

"For Yours is the kingdom and the power and the glory forever"

These are the priorities of the kingdom of God. It is His kingdom; therefore, we seek first the kingdom of God and His righteousness. It is His Power and without Him we can do nothing, but through Christ we can do all things. It is His Glory and we pray that when men see our good works they will glorify our Father who is in Heaven.

"Amen!"

This is the verification of our faith, affirming all that we have prayed for and asking God to make it so. Amen means to "let it be so." *"All the promises of God in Him are Yes, and in Him Amen."*[4]

Although this is the model for daily prayer, taught by our Lord Himself, it is only the beginning of our prayer journey. It is just the foundation of prayer. From this fundamental platform we can begin to go deeper in the things of God through a fuller revelation of prayer and intercession. Faith will take us higher and further than we have ever gone in our communion with the Lord.

PRAYING ONE HOUR

In my journey of learning to pray the prayer of faith, I was dramatically influenced by Dr. David Yonggi Cho's teaching and emphasis on prayer. His book on the *Fourth Dimension*, a Christian classic, was a powerful force in my thinking about prayer and faith. His book, *Prayer that Brings Revival*, is also very motivating. I remember his now-famous statement: "Something supernatural happens when you pray one hour." His million-member church in Korea, Yoido Full Gospel Church, has modeled intense and serious prayer for the world and the Body of Christ. Every day, thousands of Korean believers are praying fervently on Prayer Mountain, in special services and in cell groups. Could it be any coincidence that the largest church in the history of the world is also perhaps the greatest praying church? His people have translated Dr. Cho's electrifying faith and vision into detailed and focused prayer. This kind of concerted prayer effort has brought about a congregation that is renowned around the globe. Prayers of pinpointed accuracy become the agents that bring vision to pass.

If we will give ourselves to an hour of prayer every day, we will discover an entire new world of the Spirit that will amaze us. Our faith is implemented through prayer. The first preacher to pray with me for one hour was Pastor Fred Kropp who is now on our staff in Seattle. He and I have been friends since our college days during the Jesus revolution that took place in the early seventies. I was preaching for him years ago when he and his wife Pam were pastoring in Missouri. Fred and I went to the church office very early before his two Sunday services were scheduled to begin. He pulled up two chairs beside his desk, knelt down, and began to pray. We prayed, on our knees, for one hour. When church started, we were ready. There was a marvelous freedom there that could be directly attributed to our prayers. During those same years, as I learned to pray the Lord's prayer and spend more time in the presence of the Lord, I found many things to be new for me. I had more energy during the day. My attitude was greatly improved. Problems and people did not easily disturb me and things just worked out better during my daily routines. I had more grace, peace, strength, and favor. I also experienced what it was like to become addicted to His presence and grace and then miss it for a day. The contrast was horrific. I have only allowed that to happen a few times. Once we experience the grace that flows through us after learning to pray, we will be gripped by its impact on our lives and never again want to live without it.

HONEST TO GOD PRAYER

We cannot impress God. We cannot fool Him or convince Him of our spirituality. Some believers pray religious and formal prayers as if to impress God and then blurt out their real feelings of complaint, murmuring, or criticism to people around them. The truth is that God is the only One who can handle our true feelings, most people cannot. We should reverse the approach—blurting out our true inner feelings to God and speaking with more discretion and formality to people.

I stumbled upon this principle years ago, while still in college. I was going through a time of emotional turmoil, a common ailment of the age, and used to retreat to Kurtz Park in Nampa, Idaho late at night to cry out to God. Sometimes I yelled so loud that I wondered if I could be heard back at the dorm. I remember asking God about many things, including all the hard questions of life. I wondered if He really loved me. I questioned His work in my life. I asked why He allowed suffering. I asked why He did not reveal Himself more clearly—and all at the top of my lungs.

I learned something about God's nature. He never got mad at me, never rebuked me, and never got offended with me. I felt no guilt for my honesty. I realized that God could handle my emotions, thoughts, and questions. He was my Creator and had all the answers, even if I was confused.

Later, while reading my Bible, I came across an encouraging verse of Scripture in the Psalms. David said, *"Trust in Him at all times, you people; pour out your heart before Him; God is a refuge for us."*[5] I discovered that I could pour out my heart to the Lord and He could handle it. He was my refuge. I realized that I could not distress God because there was nothing I could tell Him that He did not already know. I could verbalize my feelings without fear. Many times, I felt like the father who brought his son to Jesus and said, *"Lord, I believe; help my unbelief."*[6]

In those days of soul searching and questioning, my faith was weak. Out of that honesty and sincerity of heart, faith continued growing. When telling the parable of the sower, Jesus described the good soil as a noble and honest heart where the seed of the Word could be planted and bring forth much fruit. God does not want us to fake it, playing the hypocrite of faith, but He wants us to be honest before Him and grow in genuine faith. We can approach God with confidence, honestly confessing our need and heart condition. At the same time, we can learn to speak faith and align our heart, emotions, and confession with the Word of God. We can learn to pray the prayer of faith.

THE SECRET PLACE

What we do in secret will be made known in public. The secrets of all men's hearts will be disclosed. The Bible says God will judge the secrets of men through Jesus Christ. God knows our hearts and the secret things belong to the Lord. He hides those who fear Him in the secret place of His tabernacle and shows them His mysteries. It is in this secret place of His presence that we are hidden from the schemes of men and God's secret counsel is shared with us. There are hidden riches in these places, and it is here that we are cleansed from secret faults. He answers us from His secret place. If we dwell in the secret place of the Most High, we will then abide under the shadow of the almighty God.

Jesus stated that when we pray, we are to go into a closet and close the door and *pray to [our] Father who is in the secret place, and [our] Father who sees in secret will reward [us] openly."*[7] The word for place is defined as "an inner chamber, a storage place, or a secret room." Every believer needs to have a holy place where he can pour out his heart before the Lord without interruption. I often wondered why Jesus talked about this room with the closed door. When we discover true heart-felt prayer and begin to spend time praying and waiting on God, we will recognize the need for a place of prayer where no one can hear us. It must be a place where we meet with God, a holy place where we can encounter the Almighty and discuss matters of the kingdom. We need to find that place, go there daily, and find that He is already there, waiting for us.

THE PRAYER OF FAITH

When the apostle James mentions the prayer of faith in the New Testament, it is in context of healing the sick. It also refers to the prayers of Elijah, who was a man of similar nature, and so effective in his supplication that he changed the weather and stopped the rains of heaven. The prayer of faith will heal the sick and save us from a walk of unbelief and fruitless living. When we approach God through prayer, we need to come with boldness and faith. When we ask the Lord for anything in prayer, believing, we will receive. Faith pleases God, and prayers of faith are like sweet-smelling sacrifices to the Lord.

The prayer of faith is the prayer that trusts God completely and attacks problems ruthlessly. The prayer of faith resists evil spirits and releases divine power. The prayer of faith stands in the gap for an unsaved loved one and persistently hopes for their conversion. The prayer of faith does not hedge its bets, just in case something does not work out. This prayer is strong and intense, fully confident in the revealed will of God through the Scriptures. This praying is bold and assured of its outcome. This prayer has the ring of authority to it and the boldness of one who knows what he is doing. The prayer of faith goes after the breakthrough, the miracle, the impossible situation, and wholly expects supernatural results. This is the kind of prayer that goes after divine healing of terminal disease. It assaults poverty and believes for a window to be opened in the heavens. The prayer of faith can heal a body, save a soul, build a church, reconcile a marriage, restore a prodigal, perform a miracle, and change the weather. Jesus said we could move mountains with just a seed of this kind of faith.

INTERCESSORS

My mother-in-law, Yvonne Hernandez, is a woman of great faith. Before Gini and I met, Mom prayed her into the will of God. She influenced Gini to return to the Nazarene college where we met in 1972. Had Mom not believed God and prayed so fervently, my life would be totally different, and I would not have found Gini—who is my best friend, closest confidante, most trusted ally, and the wisest pastor on our church staff.

Gini's passion for intercession and commitment to the power of prayer came from two great influences in her life. The closest of course was her own mother, who influenced her destiny and connection with me. The other indirect influence was her grandparents. Although they died prematurely, their heritage of prayerfulness had great impact on their children and grandchildren. They were involved in Rev. Aimee Semple McPherson's ministry in Los Angeles in 1934, driving a bus and helping to bring people to the great Angeles Temple during days of revival and anointing. I have a photograph in my office of Gini's grandfather kneeling in prayer along with a few others in the basement of his little market in Beverly Hills in the 1930's. Every time Gini stands to lead our church or intercessors group in prayer, I thank God for that godly heritage and anointing passed down to her and now on to our children and grandchildren.

There is a remarkable anointing on this generation to intercede. Prayer movements have always preceded revivals. In our century and millennia, the Holy Spirit is sweeping the world with an emphasis that is second to none of the past moves of God. Millions of believers are being touched by this fresh grace for prayer. The face of the Church will be changed and our world will be impacted by it.

In the first year of our church, I remember being frustrated on Saturday nights. The night before a service is a funny time for a pastor. He cannot let down too much, but at the same time he cannot expend too much energy because he must preach the next morning. In desperation to find a solution, I contacted some of our key servants in the church who were faithful in prayer and asked if they would join me at the church one Saturday night. We met and simply prayed for the service the next morning. It was so good we have continued it for over eight years. The Nordstroms, Catletts, Erwins, Porters, and Keplers as well as Liz, Sherry, Jacoline, Sue, and others have faithfully supported us in prayer and personal intercession over these many years. They have traveled with us, protected us, and stood by us through church and family crises, weddings, and grandchildren. I do not know how we ever lived without them.

I once told our church that we would never have less prayer, only more. By the time we moved into our new building, we were engaged in corporate prayer before Sunday and Wednesday services, at ladies prayer on Tuesdays, staff prayer on Wednesdays, and men's prayer on Saturday mornings. We soon added Prayer Watches three times a day and an intercessors gathering on Saturday nights. We are confident that many of the schemes of the Evil One that were intended against us and the church never materialized because they were stopped dead in their tracks through intercession and concerted prayer. The apostle John saw intercession in his Revelation as incense mixed with the prayers of the saints ascending before God. The intercession of the saints will be one of the great weapons of the Church at the end of time.

WHAT DO YOU WANT?

It is one of the most potent questions in the Bible and was asked of many significant people throughout the Scriptures. Some had great answers, while some were obviously unprepared for the magnitude of what they were being asked. It was the first question Jesus asked anyone in His earthly ministry. One prophet asked it of another before he was taken up into heaven in a whirlwind. It was the same question God asked Solomon in a dream. I believe it is being asked of us today as first-fruit believers of the new millennium. The question is, "What do you want?"

I recall the first time the Holy Spirit asked me the question, "What do you want?" I was naive and truly unprepared to answer judiciously.

We dream about what we want, but we really do not have a clue. At just the time I felt prepared to answer, I heard the Spirit ask, "Are you sure that's what you want?" It stopped me in my tracks. I remember thinking, "Why do you ask? Am I missing something here? Am I supposed to answer differently?" God knew some things I did not, and He was evaluating my motives and priorities. He was assessing what I really valued and challenging me to examine and search my heart carefully for the things that were most important to me. I also came to an epic conclusion—that God actually wanted to give me whatever I asked for and that I could truly have whatever I wanted. Although I knew blessings to be within the framework of God's good will, I knew I had to be careful when filling in this blank check from God.

Elijah asked the question of Elisha before he was taken up into heaven in a whirlwind. He asked the younger prophet, *"Ask, what may I do for you?"*[8] Elisha responded by asking for a double portion of Elijah's anointing, to which the elder man of God replied, *"You have asked a hard thing."*[9] But he received that double portion and consequently performed precisely twice as many miracles during his life and ministry as Elijah had. When was the last time we asked a hard thing of the Lord?

Queen Esther was asked, *"What is your petition...and what is your request?"*[10] She shrewdly responded to the king by asking for the life of her people and became the deliverer of the Jews. When the King tells us to ask, we had better be prepared to ask wisely and largely, for we may not have another opportunity.

Nehemiah was asked by his king, *"What do you request?"*[11] After praying and asking the Lord for wisdom to answer, he requested to be sent at the king's command to rebuild the walls of his city, Jerusalem. He boldly added an appeal for financial support and the needed supplies for the rebuilding process.

The Lord appeared to Solomon in a dream and said to him, *"Ask! What shall I give you?"*[12] The Lord was so delighted with his humble appeal for wisdom that He threw in riches and honor and all the rest.

The first question ever asked by our Lord Jesus happened one day as He walked by John the Baptist and two of John's disciples. The two began to follow Jesus after John called Him the Lamb of God. Jesus turned around and asked them, *"What do you seek?"*[13] They stood there almost speechless. They were staring at the Lamb of God, and He just asked them what they wanted. Think of it for a moment. They could have asked for anything. They could have asked for insight into the kingdom, a touch of His power, special revelation about His mission, or even to be His disciples. Instead, they haltingly stumbled over their words asking a short-sighted, practical question. The only thing that came out of their mouths was a request for His address. *"Where are you staying?"* [14] they inquired.

Two blind men begged for help by the side of the road. Jesus stopped and asked, *"What do you want Me to do for you?"* [15] As if it wasn't obvious. "We want to see," they responded. But they could have had more.

Two of Jesus' disciples, James and John, came to Jesus privately and asked for His favor. Jesus said, *"What do you want Me to do for you?"* [16] Their self-seeking request, prompted by their mother, was to sit on His right and left hand in the kingdom. They had no idea what they were asking or that two men had already been chosen to drink His cup with Him at the place of the skull.

In 1995, we had invited a notable pastor and his wife from the volatile city of Belfast, Northern Ireland, to minister in our church. I will never forget that Saturday night in our former rented facility. Pastor Paul and Priscilla Reid had no idea that the Lord had already directed the question to me on many occasions. While preaching, Paul paused, looked right at me, and said in his Irish brogue, "I believe the Holy Spirit is asking you, Wendell and Gini, 'What do you want?'" I began to weep as I heard the Lord speak to me through this Irish preacher. Priscilla followed, prophesying that God was going to give us what we wanted but we were to be very careful what we asked for. What does a pastor ask God for? Success? Crowds? Money? Buildings? People? I started asking for souls in our city, nation, and world. In the right priority we can ask for anything that is in the Book.

I recently watched a professional sports team win a world championship. After the game, confetti was flying, music was blaring, and fans were screaming as the team members hugged and congratulated one another. In the post-game interviews, the winners were asked how they felt. They responded with comments like, "It hasn't really sunk in yet," or, "We'll be back and win it again next year." I wanted to ask them, "Is this really what you want?" They had achieved what they were after, reaching the pinnacle of their careers, but I wondered if that was really what they wanted. How many people, even believers, are running after something that they are not really sure they want? We should ask ourselves the question, "What do I really want?"

WE CAN HAVE WHATEVER WE WANT

Just reading those words can seem strange. "We can have whatever we want!" There is something about that statement we react to. We are not quite sure we can have anything we want, even though Jesus Himself tells us to ask the Father for anything in His name. He says to ask so that our joy may be full. However, the truth is that we cannot have just anything we believe for! We can have whatever God tells us to believe for. True faith is not new-age meditation, optimistic thinking, or some marketing tool to sell a product. Faith comes by hearing a Word from God. Within the parameters of His Word, He speaks to us through the Holy Spirit and it births faith in our hearts. There are God-set limitations of faith. As we stay within them, we can ask and believe to receive.

God's desire is to give us what we ask, but first He must transform us by the new birth and we must put on His new nature. Through the processes of growth and maturity, we begin to reflect His image. In due course, we begin to ask accurately within the boundaries He has established and subsequently see answers to our petitions. Once our motives are right before God and the Word is hidden in our heart, we can ask for anything and He will give it to us, because our desires are His desires. We are virtually praying His will to be done on earth as it is in heaven. It is a great plan the Father has.

These verses of Scripture are truly staggering in their implications:

+ James 4:2: *You have not because you ask not.*
+ Matthew 7:11: *Your heavenly Father will give good things to those who ask Him.*
+ Matthew 7:8: *Everyone who asks receives, and he who seeks finds, and to him who knocks it will be opened.*

- 1 John 5:14-15: *If we ask anything according to His will...*
- James 1:6: *Ask in faith without doubting.*
- John 16:24: *Ask and you will receive that your joy may be full.*
- John 15:16: *Whatever you ask the Father in My name, He may give you.*
- John 15:7: *If you abide in Me and My words abide in you, you will ask what you desire, and it shall be done for you.*
- John 14:14: *If you ask anything in My name, I will do it.*
- Mark 11:24: *Whatever things you ask when you pray, believe that you receive them, and you will have them.*
- Matthew 18:19: *If two of you agree on earth concerning anything that they ask, it will be done for them by My Father in heaven.*
- Ephesians 3:20: *He is able to do exceedingly abundantly above all that we ask or think.*

Faith speaks. The word of faith is in our mouths. We must know what we want and then verbalize it in prayer and daily conversation. We must not hold back. Instead, we should ask largely of God. He is our good heavenly Father and will give us whatever we need. We can pray the prayer of faith and watch what He will do.

THE FUNDAMENTALS

Years ago, I coached my daughter's high school basketball team. Our record was dismal and the greatest challenge was teaching those raw recruits the basics of basketball. We spent weeks just dealing with ball-handling, going over and over the same fundamentals of basketball every practice. Dribbling, passing, shooting, and rebounding were all rehearsed in the drills. To that point in my life, I had never seen a basketball player cry because they were tired of running. They worked at it, though, and we pulled together some semblance of a team. The games were the reward—some of them anyway. Even NBA stars have to practice the fundamentals every day—they are that important.

Golf also takes practice time and great concentration. That is one of the reasons I like it. I have to forcibly put other things out of my mind and focus on hitting that little white ball. Sometimes it is maddening. I am supposed to hit the ball straight and fairly long. I must keep my

135

head still and at the same time position my feet in the right direction—all the while swinging the club properly. And no matter what the outcome, I am expected to exercise self-control and patience. It sounds so easy. I have no expectation to be Tiger Woods. I am just a man who is practicing his sanctification on the golf course. But even Tiger has to practice. In fact, he does it more than most and that may be a key to his success.

If we are going to excel in faith, we must adhere to the fundamentals of the faith. We are not just speaking of repentance, water baptism, or other foundational truths, assuming that every believer has laid that kind of solid foundation in Christ. We are referring to growing in faith by using the primary principles of the kingdom and employing them daily to become healthy, happy, redemptive faith-people. Here are the Christian fundamentals we all need to work on:

1. Bible—read your Bible every day. Put the Scriptures before television in your home. Meditate on God's Word day and night by reading through the entire Bible annually. Pray the Scriptures out loud as you spend time before the Lord. Build your knowledge of the Word and allow your faith to grow.
2. Prayer—access the grace you need every day through prayer, going boldly to the throne of grace. Wait on the Lord in prayer and worship and listen to the inner voice of the Holy Spirit. Commune with the Lord daily and constantly, allowing your needs and the concerns of others to be known to Him.
3. Church—do not miss it. Set aside the first day of the week for a celebration of the Resurrection and seek first the kingdom of God and His righteousness. Go to special gatherings and receive impartation from every genuine faith source possible. The church is the equipping and training center for the kingdom of God. It is where we go to be prepared for more effective ministry and fruitful living and is a place for sweet and godly fellowship.
4. Giving—pay your tithes. Go beyond tithing to giving in offerings, giving to the poor, and to brothers or sisters in need. Let liberality become a lifestyle—giving generously, blessing others, helping a

person in need, paying the bill, and tipping largely–making some-one's day.

5. Serving–find a place of service in your local church. Focus your faith on the realities of daily life with those around you. No one needs training to be a blessing. No one needs permission to love others and be a witness of the life of Jesus. There are many things you can do to help strengthen your local church, support your pas-tor, and find fulfillment at the same time. Do not strive to find a ministry, just begin by serving and helping others. Remember, it is by losing your life that you find it.

6. Confession–use the words of God, weaving them into your daily conversation. Set a watch by your lips and guard what you say. Speak life not only to those around you but also to yourself. Your mouth reveals your level of faith, for *"out of the abundance of [your] heart,"*[17] what you really believe, your mouth speaks. You should not use your words to just describe your situation, but rather use your words to change your situation. The apostle James described the tongue as a rudder on a ship. Utilize your confession to set your course into the great waters of faith and fruitfulness.

7. Attitude–joy is a choice. Determine to be a happy faith-representa-tive of Jesus. Many believers are far too intense and serious about life. Some are even grumpy, while others whine and murmur. This is not the way the Lord intended us to live. Although the stakes of heaven and hell are a serious matter, and the realities of the fear of God are genuine, the Lord has given us Good News as our message and wants to fill us with joy in fulfilling His will. *"In [His] presence is fullness of joy."*[18] We are to offer the sacrifices of joy and thanksgiv-ing. Jesus was anointed with joy above His peers, and He expects us to share that same anointing. Believers should be the happiest peo-ple on earth. They should be filled with joy and rejoice in the Lord always. The joy of the Lord should be their strength and even in the testing or persecution of their faith, they are exhorted by the Scriptures to rejoice and be exceeding glad. We should not be aggravated, agitated, anxious, fretful, or uptight, but at peace and full of His joy. Stir up that peace and joy and let faith guide your demeanor. Your personality can change. You can improve and grow

by the transformation that occurs as you renew your mind, alter your confession, discipline your attitude, and enjoy the adventure of serving the Lord.

Jesus exhorted, *"take heed how you hear."* [19] The Bible tells us, *"man shall not live by bread alone; but...by every word that proceeds from the mouth of the Lord."* [20] In Greek this Scripture is written in the present tense and could be translated, "live by every *rhema*-word that is proceeding out of the mouth of God!" The Word of God is the source of our faith. If we want to grow in our faith, we must be committed to some lifestyle changes that will assist us to that end.

We will never have great faith by simply hoping for it or by confessing some presumptuous slogan over and over again. True faith only comes from one source—the Word of God (the Bible) and the inspiration of the Holy Spirit upon it. If one does not read the Word, the Holy Spirit has limited means of communication in which to speak a *rhema*-word to us. God communicating with us is never the problem; the problem is our receivers are not tuned in to His frequency. We are dull of hearing.

5:04

It happened to me for several weeks in a row. I was so slow to grasp what the Lord was doing. Every morning I would awaken, turn over, and glance at the digital clock, and the time would be exactly 5:04 AM. The alarm was not sounding, and no disturbance had startled me. I saw no vision, just the digits on the clock—5:04. I tried rebuking the Devil but I still kept waking up at 5:04. This reoccurred at least ten times before I caught on. Finally, I lay there wide-awake and asked the Lord, "Father, what is the problem?" I was surprised to hear a quick response in my spirit, "Look it up." I paused, wondering if I was hearing things. *Look what up?* I thought. Then, as the sun was coming up, it dawned on me. It was a Scripture reference.

I had several options: chapter 5, verse 4; chapter 50, verse 4; or page 504. I started with chapter 50 since there are only four of them in the Bible—Genesis, Psalms, Isaiah, and Jeremiah. I flipped the pages of my Bible to Isaiah and had to look no further. As I read it out loud to myself I began to weep, *"The Lord GOD has given me the tongue of the learned, that I should know how to speak a word in season to him who is weary. He awakens me morning by morning, He awakens my ear to hear as the learned."*

The Lord was so graciously and patiently trying to communicate His Word and His direction to my spirit. He desired to meet with me every morning, show me His new mercies, refresh me, and guide me with His eye. I was humbled. I was ashamed and embarrassed before Him. I repented and asked the Lord to wake me every morning whenever He wanted to speak to me.

We are His faith-representatives on the planet. Who else can He speak to? Who else can He use to publicize His love to the earth dwellers? Who else will listen to Him and obey when He speaks? We must respond. He is always speaking. He will speak to us in the night seasons and in the day. At the breakfast table, in our car, at noon, or sitting at our desks, He will speak. He may speak through the anointing that comes upon the pages of our own Bible as we read. He may speak through a friend who shares an insight from the Lord. He may speak through a prophecy, a word of knowledge, or an anointed exhortation at a church gathering. He may speak to us through the lyrics of an inspired modern psalm while our hands are extended and our heart is fully engaged in worship. He may speak to us through nature, through the heart of a child, through a sign on the roadway, or through a cloud in the heavens. He may come to us with that still small voice of the Spirit in our inner man, or He may even awaken us with a digital clock and communicate His love. We will know His voice. We will know His Spirit. We will recognize His presence. He will come, and faith will come with Him. We are the ones He has chosen to represent Him so that the whole world can hear what God is saying today. What a privilege!

ASKING IN FAITH

If I delight myself in Him, He will give me the desires of my heart. Whatever I ask, He will give me because I delight in Him. I will ask and receive that my joy may be full. Whatever I ask in His name, He will give it to me. If I ask anything according to His will, I know that He hears me and if He hears me, I know that I will have the requests that I have desired of Him. I will ask largely and believe.

He will grant all my petitions, fulfill all my desires, and answer all my prayers. So whatever things I ask when I pray, I believe that I receive them and I shall have them. Until now, I have asked nothing in His name. Whatever I ask the Father in Jesus' name He will give me.

HE IS THE GOD WHO ANSWERS PRAYER

He is the God who answers by fire. He is Abba Father, our Advocate, the Amen, the Bishop of our souls, the Consolation of Israel. He is the Forerunner who has gone inside the veil for us as an anchor of hope. He is the Friend that sticks closer than a brother. He is the God Who Forgives, the God who performs all things for us, and the God who sees.

He is Jehovah Maccaddeshem—the Lord our Sanctifier; Jehovah Rapha—the Lord our Healer; Jehovah Shammah—the Lord who is present; and Jehovah Tsidkenu—the Lord our Righteousness. He is the Lily of the Valley and the Rose of Sharon. He is the Lord who dwells between the cherubim, My Portion forever, My Redeemer, the Physician, the Potter, the High Priest, the Propitiation, and the Purifier. He is the Rabbi, the Refiner, and the Righteous Judge.

When I pray, I receive the Spirit of Adoption, the Spirit of Grace, the Spirit of Holiness, the Spirit of Knowledge, and the fear of the Lord. He is the Strength of my heart, the True Vine, the One who hears prayer and saves those who trust in Him.

The Faith Age

"Thus I will magnify Myself and sanctify Myself, and I will be known in the eyes
of many nations. Then they shall know that I am the LORD."
Ezekiel 38:23

And the name of the Lord Jesus was magnified.
Acts 19:17

The clouds roll back, the heavens tear in two like a sheet of blue paper,
a loud and prolonged trumpet blast splits the air as blazing light
pierces every dark corner of the globe. The ground underneath our feet
begins to tremble. The mountains are melting like wax. Every living,
breathing thing on the face of the earth stops in its tracks, looking
upward. Automobiles roll to a halt. Computers freeze. Cell phones die.
Cash registers lock. Skyscrapers rock. Stadiums empty. Every human
sound chokes in silence. Angelic hosts suddenly become visible.
Exposed demons run for cover. Sinful men call for rocks to fall on them.
Graves burst open and glorified bodies shoot into the sky like missiles.
Rare colored beams of light form a stairway from space to earth. A
heavenly Being of indescribable beauty and authority begins to
descend out of heaven. Heavenly horsemen accompany Him with an
innumerable host of cosmic light creatures. The single most cata-
clysmic event in the history of the world is unfolding. Jesus Christ is
returning to the planet.

WILL HE FIND FAITH ON THE EARTH?

When He comes, He will be looking for faith. The eyes of the Lord will run back and forth throughout the whole earth looking for those whose hearts are right toward Him. His chaste eyes will sweep the nations and comb the barrios, scan the cities and explore the villages, inspect the streets and visit the sanctuaries. His piercing eyes will scrutinize every secret place, investigate every hidden thing, and evaluate every camouflaged soul. He will be scanning for faith, searching for believers, probing for genuine conviction. Faith detectors and holy radar will pinpoint the locations of people of faith. We might be surprised. We might be shocked. We might even be embarrassed. A child here, an elderly widow there, a street person, a prostitute, a beggar, a mental patient, an aids victim, a heroin addict, a wealthy CEO—all may be vessels of faith. Only God knows these things. Only God can peer into human hearts and identify genuine faith. Only He can judge. Simple, vital, elementary faith—that is what He will be looking for. One moment of trust in His mercy, one twinkle of faith in the eye of a dying soul, one cry from the heart of an unregenerate, one sincere reach of faith from a seeker, and He hears their cry. He knows their hearts and He answers their prayers. He loves faith. He searches for it. He honors it. He revels in it. He throws parties when He finds it. He is looking for faith. Will He find it in us?

THE FAITH-REPRESENTATIVES

Most earth dwellers know little of the One who dwells in the heavens. God is looking for believers on the planet to properly represent Him to the other inhabitants. We act on His behalf. We are His advocates, salesmen, and work force on the globe. We are His campaigners, activists, and ambassadors. As believers we are faith-representatives. It is our mission, duty, and commission to stand for Him before unbelievers and searchers of truth. We are the faith-people, the representatives of the eternal kingdom of God.

Every church is a kingdom franchise, every pastor a manager, and every believer a sales representative of that kingdom. It is the kingdom of faith. We represent the Name to those who have never heard it, to those who do not know its power, and even to those who abuse it. The Lord searches the earth to find someone whose heart is right to properly represent Him to people who have no faith.

The whole purpose of our life as faith-representatives is to help people believe in the Lord Jesus Christ and be saved. Some people believe that this life is all there is and that when we die, it is all over. Others believe there is some kind of good afterlife that everyone will enjoy. Many believe in a religion of works that demands duty and deeds to prove our worthiness to some demanding deity. Still others have embraced religions that teach the worship of other gods, which are, in actual fact, demons. Some worship themselves and the human body, creating their own gods. These philosophies and religions cannot produce good fruit. They are bad trees. They are wolves in sheep's clothing. They are falsehoods. They are empty lies. They are demonic deceptions. They will leave people empty, unhappy, and eternally separated from God and His matchless love.

God is looking for faith-representatives in the grocery store, the mall, our neighborhoods, the classroom, on the basketball court, and out on the golf course. God is looking for faith-representatives in the halls of justice and in the leadership of nations. He is looking for a faith-representative on the cruise, in the airplane, and on the bus. He wants them on television, on the radio, on the phone, in the mail, and is even searching cyber space to find His faith-representatives who will stand up for truth, purity, and Good News. And surely the Head of the Church is looking for faith-representatives in His own house, the church.

FAITH-PEOPLE

When the apostle Paul wrote to Timothy, he spoke much of faith. He declared that Jesus Christ was *"believed on in the world."*[1] God is looking for those who will believe on Him while surrounded by all the contradictions of faith in today's world. The Lord searches for true faith-people, those who will trust in the invisible, supernatural work of a benevolent and eternal God.

What does a person of faith look like? What qualities describe this kind of life form? What characteristics should we pursue? This faith-person is peaceful, with a quiet confidence in God and His Word. He or she speaks well of people and speaks positive, faith-filled words about life and situations. He or she has a good attitude and a godly demeanor. This person is generous, giving, and liberal with finances. He or she has a good sense of humor and knows how to rejoice and enjoy the good things God has given us. The hallmarks of faith-representatives are clear. They are what others want to be:

- Purpose seekers
- History makers
- People builders
- Life talkers
- Joy producers
- Truth speakers
- Demon busters
- Promise keepers
- Mountain climbers
- Water walkers

We are faith-people. We breathe a different air. We eat a different food. We drink from a different source. We are dressed in different garments. Our eyes see different things. Our ears hear different voices. We sleep a different sleep and dream a different dream. We are those who have been redeemed from earth-bound elements and have received the deposit of the divine—the God-shaped nature. We have been born from above, by the Spirit. We have been baptized into His death and resurrected by His power. We have been filled with the awesome and blessed Holy Spirit. We have tasted the heavenly gift and become partakers of the age to come. We have been empowered and enabled by the supernatural gifts of heaven. We were given tongues of fire and hearts that flow with living water.

We are the faith-people. We meditate on God's precepts and all our ways are being changed. We follow the directives of the Captain of the Lord's hosts and have been commissioned by the Master Himself to go global and propagate His miraculous message. We have been entrusted with the greatest news anyone has ever heard. We are anointed to tell people that they can escape the gravitational pull of sin forces. We are empowered to open prison doors, call out captives, be spiritual exchangers, and trade the commodities of heaven for the slag of earth. There have never been a people like this on the planet. We have been around for two millennia, multiplied, and are now covering the earth with the communiqué of the kingdom. We are the faith-people. We are the ones He is looking for and the ones He is coming for. He expects much from us. His investment will not be in vain. He will not be disappointed. Faith-people will be ready when He returns. Faith-people will believe Him and do exploits. We are the people of faith.

TREASURE IN EARTHEN VESSELS

Grace is the heavenly influence that qualifies us to be used of God. It is the gift of God that we receive by faith. It is the means of our salvation and the enabler of our walk of faith. It is the power of God within us that enables us to perform the will of God. It is the message of the New Covenant established by our Lord Jesus, having sealed it with His own blood. He died for our sins, wiping out the judgment against us and qualifying us for His service. He decided to use humans to service and build His Church. Although we might have chosen angels, He chose man who is higher than the animals and a little lower than the angels.

The Bible says that God uses us even in our weakness. In fact, when we are weak, we are especially strong because that is when the power of Christ rests upon us. We should not be disheartened, wondering whether or not God will use us. He will. He wants to. He delights to. It is His good pleasure to give us the kingdom. It is His pleasure to overlook our faults, cover our sins, compensate for our weaknesses, and anoint our strengths. He is glorified when we do great things in His name. The treasure of God is wrapped in an earthen vessel so that the glory goes to Him. He is magnified when we are employed to extend His rule in the earth.

King David illustrated the depth of God's grace when He declared that the Lord had anointed his horn with fresh oil. He recognized that the Lord was anointing his strengths while at the same time covering his weaknesses. As believers, we are to do the same for one another, since the Scriptures admonish us to let love cover a multitude of sins and confess our faults to one another. This is sealed by a prayer of faith that brings healing, not only to the individual, but also to the Body of Christ.

I often remind our staff, "You wouldn't have the privilege of being frustrated by my weaknesses if it wasn't for my strengths!" In other words, if not for the gift of God in me to gather people, preach the Gospel, and rally people together for the kingdom of God, we would have had no reason to employ them! My weaknesses are many, but that is the purpose for our talented staff—to compensate for my lack. We celebrate one another's giftings and graces and cover for one another's weaknesses.

All of us have been hurt, or at least disappointed, by another believer somewhere along the way. The Church is human and has its flaws, but our collective humanity becomes a collage of gifts as well as faults. Therefore, there must be love. There must be graciousness. There must be a covering. There must be forgiveness, much patience, and forbearance shown by all, treating one another the way we would want to be treated by classifying our weaknesses and publishing our strengths.

THE FAITH AGE

The era of faith is on the horizon. Not everyone will backslide or fall away. There are many people standing fast in the faith and running the race with endurance. The true believers that have genuine and sincere faith will shine forth like the sun in the kingdom of their Father. A company of overcomers will triumph by their faith and be dressed and ready when the trumpets of heaven announce the re-entry of the Bridegroom.

People who have called themselves followers of Christ but do not know Him, love Him, or keep His commandments will be known. Those who call Him "Lord" but do not obey Him, live lawless lives, are hearers but not doers of the Word, and have a form of godliness but deny the power—these people will be exposed. Truth will prevail. Shafts of heavenly light will spotlight everything hidden in the dark. Things whispered in back rooms of wickedness will be shouted from rooftops of righteousness. God will judge sin, and all those who insist on harboring the rebel element in their hearts will go down with it. Some will repent, but others will harden their hearts against God and true holiness.

The faith age will soon come upon us. It will be the season of history where faith will be manifest as the treasure of the human experience. It will be validated as the authentic wealth of life before all mankind. Those who have invested in the bank of heaven and the stock market of the Spirit will visibly reap dividends that make the nations rage with envy. The time of faith is coming. It will be the time when true believers will rejoice in their great salvation and charlatans will cower and flee in fear. This era will justify the faithful and rectify inequity. It will be the culmination of the plan and purpose of God. This will be the time when faith will be honored and the faithful will abound with the blessings that have been stored up for them over time. We should lift up our heads as faith-people for our redemption is drawing near.

This era will see the Church become what the Lord has always intended her to be. She will be the resplendent and prepared Bride, made ready for the marriage supper. She will be the exquisite Body of Christ with every member functioning in harmony and grace. She will be the army of God, equipped with *"the whole armor of God"*[2] and ready for battle. She will be the City of Zion, adorned, beautified and coming down out of heaven. She will be the fruitful Vineyard with clusters of fruit that will bring glory to the Husbandman. She will be the House of God that is built by wisdom, established by understanding, and decorated with the treasures of knowledge. She will be the Tabernacle, the Temple, the Dwelling place of God, *"the joy of the whole earth"*[3]–the Church that Jesus built, against which the gates of hell cannot prevail. She will be the faithful one–the glorious Church filled with faithful believers, anointed and ready to finish the race of faith and complete the historical plan of God. The faith-filled ones of earth will join with the faithful cloud of witnesses of heaven and together rejoice in the greatness and goodness of their God.

Without trying to explain the millennium or attempting to detail the events preceding the coming of Christ, we simply believe that the power of the Gospel will have widespread influence and make a worldwide impact before our Lord returns. No one really knows what the last days hold for the believer and for mankind. But we have partial understanding of the end of the age from Jesus' prophecy and John's revelation. The day is yet to come when spiritual seals will be broken and a full revelation of God's strategy will come to the Body of Christ.

The heavenly Farmer waits for the precious fruit of the earth. The *"Lord of the harvest"*4 will have His yield of souls. He will return for *"a glorious church not having spot or wrinkle or any such thing."*5 The day of the Lord will not overtake us *"as a thief in the night,"* since we are *"children of the day"*6 according to Paul's letter to the Thessalonians. Things will not get worse for the believer, but better. Paul says, *"evil men and imposters will grow worse and worse, deceiving and being deceived,"*7 but for the faith person, his path will shine brighter and brighter until the coming day.

This dramatic era of faith will have several marks of distinction:

- Faith for the impossible—believing God for impossible situations, needed miracles, and spectacular breakthroughs for the sake of the Name of Christ.
- Faith for miracles—faith to perform wonders, signs, creative miracles, raising of the dead, and dramatic and creative healings of infirmity and disease.
- Faith for supernatural harvest—people being converted, changed, and transformed; hard cases delivered from darkness to light, from the power of the Devil to the power of God, and from demonic influence and oppression.
- Faith for revival and spiritual outpouring—God visiting churches, renewing and blessing them with fresh grace for the work of the ministry.
- Faith for energy and strength—supernatural strengthening of our physical bodies to enable us to accomplish the many challenging things that God has commissioned us to do.
- Faith for anointing—dramatic increases of the anointing to operate with divine power in the spiritual gifts of the Holy Spirit.
- Faith for favor—increased influence in our cities through good works and the meeting of tangible needs in our communities.
- Faith for miraculous provision—supernatural finances, facilities, and resources to be invested into the work of the church and the extension of the kingdom of heaven.
- Faith for other ministries—honoring of other churches, pastors,

leaders, and ministries, so the full, unified expression of the kingdom of God might be made manifest.

+ Faith for faith–renewed confidence in our mighty God and His powerful Word, believing for everything that He has promised to be demonstrated in our generation.

RED SKY AT NIGHT

My dad, who served in the South Pacific with the United States Navy at the end of World War II, used to repeat an old sailor's adage, "Red sky in morning, sailors, take warning; red sky at night, sailor's delight." Some are enamored with the red morning sky while others focus on the red evening sky. Focusing on the coming blessings with a faith-filled optimism for the last days is far more beneficial than concentrating on the impending doom!

The Old Testament prophets prophesied of a glorious last days Church that will manifest the glory of God and experience an outpouring of the Holy Spirit with powerful anointing. It will also be an exalted Church that attracts multiple nationalities of people and reaps a supernatural harvest of souls. Peter preached in Acts three that the heavens must receive Christ *"until the times of the restoration of all things, which God has spoken by the mouth of all His holy prophets since the world began."*[8] He said all the prophets *"from Samuel and those who follow, as many as have spoken, have also foretold these days."*[9] Catch a glimpse of the prophets' perspectives of the last days:

+ David–Psalms 102:13: *The set time of favor will come to God's people.*
+ Isaiah–2:2: *The mountain of the house of the Lord will be exalted.*
+ Jeremiah–31:13: *The virgin of the church will rejoice in the dance with both young and old together.*
+ Lamentations–5:21: *The Lord will restore us and renew our days.*
+ Ezekiel–37: *An exceeding great army of dry bones will be raised up.*
+ Ezekiel–47: *A river of life will give life wherever it goes.*
+ Daniel–10: *The glorious man will fight against our enemies.*
+ Hosea–3:5: *People will fear the Lord and His goodness in the latter days.*
+ Hosea–6:2: *After two days He will revive us and we will live in His sight.*

- Joel—2: *God will raise up a great army, send a great outpouring of the Spirit on all flesh, and show great wonders in the heavens and in the earth.*
- Amos—9:11: *The tabernacle of David will be raised up.*
- Amos—9:13: *The plowman will overtake the reaper.*
- Obadiah—17: *There will be deliverance on Mount Zion.*
- Jonah—3:10: *Whole cities will repent.*
- Micah—4:2: *He will teach us His ways and we will walk in His paths.*
- Nahum—2:3-4: *The chariots will run like lightning with flaming torches in the day of His preparation.*
- Habakkuk—2:2: *The vision will be written and plain and people will run with it.*
- Zephaniah—3:14: *The daughter of Zion will sing, shout, and rejoice.*
- Haggai—2:9: *The glory of the latter temple shall be greater than the former.*
- Zechariah—10:1: *The Lord will send rain in the time of the latter rain.*
- Malachi—3: *He will suddenly come to His temple, purify the sons of Levi, and open the windows of heaven.*
- Malachi—4:2: *The Sun of Righteousness shall arise with healing in His wings.*

There are many indicators of the end of the age and the imminent return of Christ. Not all are positive. As the Church grows in her glory and brightness so the world and its systems will increase in their darkness and delusion. Widespread deception and false Christs with demonic teachings will be a primary sign of the end of days. Jesus often warned of this kind of deception when He spoke to His disciples of the end of the age and of the signs that would indicate the approach of that era. Paul prophesied that people would turn their ears away from the truth and be turned aside to fables. I believe that the only way people would sit under demonic instruction and listen to myths, fables, and fantasies is if such teaching were cloaked so attractively in modern displays of light and sound that people would be spellbound and drawn to listen. Today's television, videos, and cinemas can be perpetrators of this kind of subtle deception, leading even God's elect astray. Faith-people must be guarded.

Paul warned Timothy that men would be *"lovers of themselves"* and *"lovers of pleasure"*[10] in days that would be marked as perilous and stressful. *"Men's hearts [will be] failing them for fear"*[11] because of the events on earth. Men will make war as nation rises against nation and king against king.

There will be signs in the heavens and on earth that will demonstrate the groaning of creation, including earthquakes, famines, diseases, and pestilence spreading in various places around the world. It is prophesied that *"stars will fall from heaven,"*[12] not unlike some of the special effects in recent movies used to depict such apocalyptic events. Jesus said in Matthew twenty-four that *"the powers of the heavens [would] be shaken."*[13]

The Bible describes a period when knowledge will be increased and many will run to and fro. The prophet Isaiah may have been describing jet airplane travel, speaking of those *"who fly like a cloud, and like doves to their roosts."*[14] The Scriptures seem to also describe automobiles when the prophet Nahum explained what he saw in his vision of chariots with torches on them, jostling in the streets and running like lightning in the day of His preparation.

The clearest and most important sign will no doubt be the preaching of the Gospel of the kingdom in all the nations, as a witness, before the end comes. Thank God for churches, evangelistic ministries, and missions groups that are declaring the word of the Gospel throughout the world in these apocalyptic days. Israel will be a signpost nation as God restores and saves millions of Jewish people in fulfillment of His Word. He will bring back His originally chosen people, and as they repent in faith there will be a huge revival and harvest of souls among the people of Israel.

The Faith Age will be a time in human history unparalleled in either ancient or modern records of mankind. You and I may have the distinct privilege of being alive when all these events unfold. If the Lord tarries, then we have a mandate to prepare our children and our children's children. We must lift up our heads, the days that the prophets spoke of and the things they desired to look into are coming upon us.

THE FAITH AGE: THE GLORIOUS CHURCH

Driving by a small church on a main boulevard, I was appalled at its unkempt condition. The lawn was not mowed, the roof needed obvious repair, peeling paint appeared of a pre-World War II vintage, and hanging outside the dilapidated building was an old broken neon sign reading, "Jesus Saves." I pondered, *From what?* It was not exactly the *"light of the world"* and the *"salt of the earth."*[15] The most tragic of circumstances for this or any church is not the condition of the outside structure, but the condition of the hearts on the inside. When Jesus returns for His glorious Church, will He find faith?

Truth really does set men free, and Jesus really is building a Church against which the gates of hell cannot prevail. But some unbelieving believers profess faith and yet refuse to believe the most fundamental of truths. These are born again, professing saints who have a depressing view of the Lord's Church. They belittle the very thing that God is building by demeaning the local church and refusing to submit to God's delegated authority. They do not believe there will be a glorious Church until some millennium, or perhaps in heaven. But we will not need it then. We need it now! It would not bring the Father any glory in heaven. His desire is to let His Church shine here and now in the midst of a darkened society and corrupted culture.

Far too many doctrines are built on reactionary theology. People craft their own belief system by safeguarding themselves from a past experience that soured their opinion of the Church. They end up teaching the commandments of men and making the Word of God of no effect through their traditions. If we were to establish our doctrine of the church on the Scriptures, instead of the opinions of independent, disillusioned, or embittered souls, we might catch a vision that would rekindle our faith and lift us to new levels of hope or expectation for the Church that Jesus is building. We might get genuinely excited about the church of which we are called to be a part.

Jesus said He would build His Church. He said it would be the salt of the earth and the light of the world. I believe the words of Jesus. Paul said it would be a glorious Church without *"spot or wrinkle."*[16] I believe the Holy Spirit inspired the words of the apostle Paul. Peter called it the *"living stones [of a] spiritual house"* and *"a holy priesthood."*[17]

I believe the Holy Spirit moved Peter to write down those words. John's Revelation talks of an overcoming assembly of people of all nationalities, tribes, and languages. John's revelation, I believe, came from heaven.

When God starts something, He finishes it. The inception of the Church was marvelous and spectacular. Surely the end will be even better. *"Better is the end of a thing than the beginning."*[18] The Lord prophesied that *"the glory of this latter house shall be greater than of the former."*[19] The Church of the last days will be a dazzling display of God's glory and purpose. It will be grander than a fireworks exhibit exploding to celebrate one of man's achievements or holidays. It will be more spectacular than the world's largest waterfall. It will be more historic than the birthing of a nation. It will be greater in its end than in its beginning. The Church of the last days will be greater than the one found in the book of the Acts of the Apostles. His Church will be stunning, impressive, extravagant, magnificent, and brilliant. It will explicitly display the spectacular power of the inimitable One.

The Church will be the reflection of the Father's glory. It will be a revelation of His nature. The Church is the apple of His eye. It is the joy of His entire eternal scheme. It is the full expression of His purpose on the earth. It is the epitome of His intention in the history of man. This Church, the work of almighty God, will be viewed by the nations, and they will exclaim, "He does all things well." He only does wondrous things. Who can fathom the works of His hands? Surely they are a people the Lord has blessed. Behold, it is very good!

THE FAITH AGE: A QUICK WORK

Many of us were watching, with both amazement and a little apprehension, as the celebrations of the Year 2000 circled the globe on New Years Eve 1999. So much had been made of the "Y2K" bug that most had some expectation of disaster awaiting us at the strike of twelve midnight. As it turned out, the most explosive things that occurred were the firework displays televised from major cities of the world. As the cameras recorded it, the celebrations moved from one time zone to another until the entire world was enraptured with this historic moment. Since the time of Christ, only one other generation has witnessed the turning of a thousand-year era.

Reflecting on the implications of globally televised festivities happening all over the world while millions, perhaps billions, of people watched, I contemplated what it would be like when revival and harvest sweep across the planet just before Christ returns. I have always been enchanted with the thought of what God could do and how speedily He could bring it to pass when the time is at hand. It was true for Abraham, Noah, Moses, Joshua, David, John the Baptist, the early church apostles, and even Jesus Himself. When God gets ready to move, He moves quickly. He could pour out His Spirit on all flesh, and His glory could cover the earth as the waters cover the sea. He could bring about worldwide harvest in a very short time. The Bible tells us He will do a quick work and *"cut it short in righteousness."* [20]

THE FAITH AGE: HEALING CHURCHES

The day will come when faith-filled, Bible-believing churches will have services and gatherings where everyone who comes in sick leaves healed. It will be similar to the days when all who came to Jesus were healed and as many as touched Him were made well of their diseases. The Holy Spirit will be poured out, and the gifts of healing that were originally given to the Church will be restored. People, believers and unbelievers alike, will seek out life-giving churches to be healed of their infirmities.

We are waiting and believing for that sickness-subduing, cancer-canceling, disease-destroying, aids-annihilating, glorious Church of the twenty-first century. This is the Church that Jesus has always desired, a glorious Church under the unction of the anointing. The lame will walk home. The blind will read the street signs heading back to their houses. The deaf will hear the sounds of praise and worship for the first time. The epileptic will be free. The Alzheimer's patients will leave restored. We are waiting for that faith Church to arise.

THE FAITH AGE: THE MIRACLE GENERATION

Several years ago, my wife and I were two of over twenty thousand people in a large indoor soccer stadium in La Plata, Argentina. We were part of a contingent of hundreds attending a South American conference on revival with Harvest Evangelism. Out of that entire gathering my wife and I were called to the platform by a well-known prophetess. When she prophesied, it was like thunder to our hearts. Laying her hands on us, she trumpeted the message into our souls, "The dead will be raised, they will line up ambulances outside your church, miracles will happen!"

We returned from that trip to discover one of our church members had died after a long battle with cancer. In obedience to the Lord, we prayed over him and believed that God would raise him from the dead. During those days of wrestling with the spirit of death, I realized the dead would never be raised unless someone prays over them. During the funeral a few days later, and to my surprise, I found that the people's faith was actually encouraged by our battle even though the brother had not been raised up. We received encouraging emails, faxes, and messages from all over the world, since we had contacted many friends and asked them to believe with us during those days. They relayed to us how their faith was strengthened just to hear that we had dared to pray for a man to be raised from the dead. One sister in our church commented, "Wow, what kind of church is this, where they keep praying for you even after you die?" Though it was a hard and difficult time for me emotionally, I knew God was stretching our faith to believe that the dead will be raised—and we will do it! I have met a few amazing individuals who have actually raised the dead, and there will be more. Great faith will be made manifest and miracles will happen.

The early church was a miracle church. The lame were healed. The dead were raised. Demons were cast out. Coming under the shadow of Peter, people were healed as he walked by. Handkerchiefs were taken from Paul, placed on the sick, and became the agents of healing to them. God used that mighty first-generation Church by multiplying it greatly and sending it to turn the world upside down.

He is going to do it again with the last-day Church of passionate men and women who will believe Him for miracles. Signs will follow those who believe as they lay hands on the sick and see them recover. They will speak with new tongues. They will have power over the Devil and cast out demons. They will raise the dead. The gift of miracles will be a hallmark of the final generation. Through their faith they will suspend natural laws and perform mighty signs in the name of Christ.

Creative miracles will occur. Limbs will grow, blind eyes will open, organs will be regenerated, cancer will be cured, AIDS will be annihilated, and the dead will be raised to life again. There is a generation that God is preparing who will have this kind of faith.

THE FAITH AGE: TRUE SHEPHERDS AND SERVANTS

At the same time, the Holy Spirit is looking for equippers and mentors—men and women of God who love people and His goal to raise up a glorious Church. Jesus will not return for an organization. He is not coming back for a stadium rally. He will be looking for a faith-filled Church. He wants a family. He wants children. He wants a love-based, Spirit-filled, Bible-believing family of brothers and sisters who are committed to Him and each other, and will hold each other accountable for righteousness and faith.

Every preacher should have faith in his mouth. The task of a minister is to build people's faith from the Word of God by speaking simple truth, feeding faith, and edifying all. According to Romans the tenth chapter, every preacher must have a word of faith in his or her mouth, in order for those who hear to believe. Bishops and overseers of churches must be filled with faith, love God's people, exalt God's Word, and extol the Lord Jesus Christ to both bless and adjust God's people.

Too many preachers are negative—down on people, down on life, and even down on faith. When standing against sin and the Devil, it is possible to preach an edifying, faith-filled message and build people up while exposing their sin to the light of the truth. Some churches practice indiscriminate radiation of sin and kill everything in sight. They employ no shields of mercy, protect no one, and unleash waves of reaction, fear, and harshness. The only people on whom Jesus ever unleashed full radiation were the unbelieving, tradition-bound, religiously-bigoted, spiritually-cocky Pharisees. If people's hearts are open and tender, even if they are filled with sin, God has a measure of faith to work with. The sick know they need a Physician. The weak know they need Strength. The faltering know they need a Refuge, and the sinners know they need a Savior. In contrast, the strong-willed, self-serving, hard-hearted, religious-thinking individual is doomed to judgment because he has cut himself off from his only hope—the mercy and love of God. To the merciful, the Lord shows Himself merciful but with the haughty He shows Himself haughty. He *"resists the proud, but gives grace to the humble."* [21]

Truth is like a laser-guided smart bomb that hits its precise and intended target. God hates and judges sin, but at the same time loves the sinner. He loved the rich young ruler but still required him to renounce his idolatry and love of money. He loved the woman taken in adultery and yet commanded her to go and sin no more. He loved the woman at the well and yet exposed her errant lifestyle. He was the friend of sinners but hated sin. He was full of grace and truth. He loved righteousness and hated lawlessness and that is why God anointed Him with the oil of joy above His companions. This same anointing is available to us today.

Deacons also must demonstrate a spirit of faith as chief servants of the Church and model true servanthood. Early church deacon qualifications included having a good reputation, being full of the Holy Spirit, and possessing wisdom. These were men and women who could handle the business of serving the growing numbers of people in the Church but were also filled with faith. Stephen, as described in the Scriptures, was a man full of faith and power. Paul, in giving Timothy the standards for deacons, mentioned how deacons can purchase great boldness in the faith through their ministry. To serve God's people in the twenty-first century Church, the deacons, or choice servants, must have faith.

THE FAITH AGE: RED AND YELLOW, BLACK AND WHITE

"Red and yellow, black and white, they are precious in His sight," these familiar words to an old Sunday school song prophesy of the forces being called out of every people group. God is raising up powerful women for His harvest, mighty young people who will believe whatever He says, strong elders who, like Caleb, will ask for mountains in the name of the Lord, even in their old age. He is raising up apostles, prophets, evangelists, and pastors and teachers. He is raising up preachers and business people. He will develop His teachers and lawyers, healers and doctors, worship leaders and artisans, intercessors and housewives. We need to get ready for the dazzling display of God's rainbow division, battalions of leaders glimmering in the light of His glory and riding strong into battle.

We must be careful and prayerful not to call common what God has called clean. The God who rebuked the apostle Peter for prejudice and bigotry will likewise deal with us. We cannot let our traditions make the Word of God of no effect and be wise in our own opinion, hindering the assembling of laborers for His ingathering of souls. When it is harvest time, it is all hands on deck. When it is wartime, everyone readies for battle. The call will go out to whosoever will. Gender, color, age, or status will not matter. Eventually the water table will rise, wash over the banks we have created, and create a mighty flow of God's love and healing anointing.

The Lord is preparing us for heaven where every nation, people, language, and tribe will be gathered. There will be ten thousand times ten thousand and thousands of thousands, a company of people, which no man can number, gathered before His throne worshipping the Lamb. It will be the Church of many colors, a Joseph company made up of God's diverse family that fellowships together for eternity. We should learn to love it now.

THE FAITH AGE: THE GREAT HARVEST OF SOULS

In the middle of an unusually anointed worship service, I felt impressed of the Holy Spirit to give an appeal for sinners and backsliders to get right with God. I knew by the Spirit there were many present that Sunday morning who needed Jesus. It became one of the longest altar calls I have ever given. I asked people to come forward. I quoted salvation and forgiveness Scriptures. I led the church in prayer. We prayed. We waited. People kept coming and the Spirit kept prompting me, "Keep going!" So I called for more to come. Over thirty people slowly made their way forward, but still the Lord would not let me conclude. Impelled by the Holy Spirit, I did something uncharacteristic and started counting down from ten to zero, telling anyone who was not right with God, they had ten seconds to respond and after that they were in God's hands. People ran to the altar and forty-three in all gave their hearts to the Lord Jesus that morning. So it will be in the last days.

Periodically we hold "Dream Sunday" where we invite everyone we can to come to our church for a Sunday morning service. I intentionally preach a short Gospel message, cast the net and believe for harvest. Saturday night, before one of these special Sundays, my wife and I stopped at Burger King on the way home from prayer. Exiting the drive-through, I rolled down my window and handed a "touch card" from our church to three young men on the street. Reluctantly, one of the guys, named Dan, took the card, joking that he usually does not take things from strangers. I used the story as an illustration in my sermon the next morning. During the altar call that same day, several people came forward and I greeted them, as I normally do, shaking their hands and asking their names. One young man enthusiastically answered, "Hi, I'm Dan from Burger King." He got saved that morning.

Our church has been experiencing what many other churches are also discovering, that people are hungry for spiritual things. Prodigals are coming back to the Father's house. Backsliders are being healed. There is a grass roots movement of the Holy Spirit that is bringing individuals back to church and God. Countless people are coming to Christ worldwide every day. No one is coordinating an effort to tabulate these results, but if the truth were known and the numbers were totaled we would probably be shocked to realize we are in the midst of a great worldwide spiritual awakening. The Holy Spirit is at work and people are coming to the Lord. Jesus is being lifted up and drawing all men unto Himself. Some of the largest gatherings in human history are happening today as millions of people are meeting to hear the Gospel preached with power.

Most of the people who surround us in our cities, communities, or neighborhoods are the multitudes in the valley of decision. Not everybody is wicked. The wicked are a minority, the few who have sold their souls for pleasure, power, or prominence. Most people are just searching, wandering, and contemplating the purpose of life. They are sincere and thoughtful people still searching for truth. If we will faithfully proclaim the Good News, most will believe and be added to the numbers of the redeemed, turning the tide of humanity and tipping the scale of souls that is being weighed out for the end of days.

"The Lord is...not willing that any should perish but that all should come to repentance."[22] He wants all men to be saved and to come to the

knowledge of the truth. He loved the world so much that *"He gave His only begotten Son, that whoever believes in Him should not perish but have everlasting life."*[23] Whoever calls on the name of the Lord in these days will be saved.

We are about to witness the greatest harvest of souls the world has ever seen. In waves of compassion, mercy, and the persuasive love of God, multitudes of people will experience the Holy Spirit being poured out abundantly on all flesh, as the Scriptures foretell. Millions of unsaved, unregenerate, unbelieving souls will believe and find peace with God. Hindus, Buddhists, Muslims, and atheists, aided by Holy Ghost divine encounters, will turn to Him. There will be jailers and sailors, presidents and prostitutes, and whole cities turning to the Lord as in the book of Acts. Men will have dreams, trances, angelic visitations, and visions of the life to come. God will have mercy on them. Multitudes will be spared a Christ-less eternity as the Spirit of God draws them into the fold of faith. Every person living and breathing on the planet in the last days will have an opportunity to believe and put his or her trust in Christ. The Holy Ghost will be poured out on all flesh—antagonistic flesh, religious flesh, resistant flesh, dying flesh, and even on wicked flesh. Not everyone will call on His blessed Name, but for those who do there will be a glorious salvation of transformed lives. The Spirit will be poured out in the dark and distant jungles and on the bright and bustling streets of every metropolis. He will visit every small town, village, marketplace, and business center. He will sweep through the schools and campuses, and He will invade concert halls and stadiums. Every child will hear the voice of God. Young people will be given opportunity to believe. The rich and the poor will both be challenged with the glorious Gospel of Jesus Christ.

In one day, millions will come to Christ. Churches of all denominations will be flooded with people seeking God. Mission organizations will be unable to keep up with the demand for materials and workers. Masses of people and whole language groups will have divine encounters and turn to the Lord. Israel will have her long awaited revival. The prayers and intercession of thousands of years will be fulfilled before our eyes as Jews become twice chosen, twice blessed, and grafted back into God's great olive tree. The beloved people of God will become followers of Jesus Christ, the true Messiah. In a supernatural invasion of eternity into time, God will have a harvest. The Husbandman will have His crop. The Son will rescue those who are perishing. The great Redeemer will purchase souls. The Cross will make its mark. The blood of the Lamb will have its effect. Jesus will gather His sheep. The Father will have His family. The Scriptures will unfold. The prophecies will be fulfilled. The Holy Spirit will be the Sower. The angels will be the reapers. The nations will be saved. Multitudes will flow to the mountain of God. The Lord will have His reward and the grand purpose of God will be accomplished. Heaven will be full.

THE FAITH AGE: THE SECOND COMING

The Second Coming of Christ is called the Blessed Hope. We are closer to it than any former generation. In fact, the generation may be living today that will have the historic privilege of occupying the planet when it transpires. The apostles expected it in their day. The Church of the second and third centuries fully expected it. At the turn of the first millennium, they were sure it was just at the next dawn; and here we are, two thousand years after Christ, still waiting, hoping, and anticipating. His return, the rapture, the end of the age, the parousia, the apocalypse, the Second Coming of Jesus Christ is on the horizon.

"Where is the promise of His coming," they cry. They have mocked the faith for two millennia. Scoffers have existed in every era. They lived, scoffed, died, and then faced the judgment of the One they scorned. Ignore the scoffers and embrace the believers. Worldwide, believers are waiting and preparing. Followers from every race, people, and language are getting ready. Jesus is coming soon and we are ready for Him!

THE FAITH AGE: ETERNAL JUDGMENT

There will be an end. God will judge the earth. He will reap the harvest of the earth in the last days. Jesus will return and all evil will be judged. No matter how we interpret the Scriptures from the Revelation of John, there is coming a full judgment against sin and wickedness. Included in that heinous list of people who qualify for fire and brimstone and everlasting torment are the cowardly and unbelieving. In Revelation chapter twenty-one and verse eight, they are listed along with the sexually immoral, murderers, sorcerers, liars, and idolaters—all the abominable ones. Right down to the final moments of earth and the judgment against sin, God will be looking for faith. If He finds one who is cowardly and lacks courage and boldness before God, or one who is still unbelieving and has no faith, they are going to be eliminated from the universe of faith. The eternal judgment of the last days will be manifest in the Church, as with Ananias and Sapphira. It is time for judgment to begin at the house of God and if it begins with us, how horrible will it be for those who do not believe the good Gospel of God? It will be a fearful time of soul searching for true believers who will be called to position themselves under the mighty hand of God in humility and holiness.

THE GOD WE BELIEVE IN

He is such a good God. He is so powerful. There is none like Him, in heaven or on earth. There is nothing too hard for Him. Nothing is impossible with our God. He is unfolding His grand and glorious intention. He is a keeper of promises. He will fulfill the prophecies. He will complete His work. Jesus Christ is *"the same yesterday, today, and forever"*[24] The Alpha is also the Omega, the beginning, and the end. He begins good works and He finishes them. He is both the *"author and finisher of our faith."*[25]

He *"works all things according to the counsel of His [own] will.""*[26] He causes all things to work together for good for those who love Him and are called according to His purpose. He is the God who gives *"beauty for ashes," "joy for mourning,"* and the *"garment of praise for the spirit of heaviness."*[27] He is the God of benefits. He is the One who forgives all our iniquities, heals all our diseases, redeems our life from destruction, crowns us with lovingkindness and tender mercies, satisfies our mouth with good things, and renews our youth like the eagle's.

The poor hear His Good News, He heals the brokenhearted, the captives are liberated, the incarcerated are set free, and the mourners are comforted. The eyes of the blind are opened, the ears of the deaf are unstopped, the lame leap like a deer, and the tongue of the mute sings praises. The Lord God blesses, anoints, helps, and heals. He comforts, cares, keeps, and covers. He guides and leads, directs and checks. He lifts up, holds on, under girds, and supports. He surrounds, protects, guards, and detects. He will go before us, come behind us, stand beside us, and never leave us.

This is the God in whom we believe. This is the One who evokes our praise. This is the One True God, the Eternal One who inspires our faith. We know Him whom we have believed, and we are persuaded that He is able to keep what we have committed unto Him, in faith, until that Day! May we magnify Him and make Him big. There is nothing He cannot do!

EXCEEDINGLY ABUNDANTLY ABOVE

God wants to stretch our faith to go beyond what we have ever done before, to believe for greater things, to imagine impossible things becoming possible, and to see the incredible become feasible and tangible in our lives. The immovable will move. The incurable will be cured. The impossible will happen. Our God is *"able to do exceedingly, abundantly, above all that we could ask or imagine, according to the power that works in us."*[28] What is it we are asking for? What is it we imagine the Lord doing for us? Whatever it is, He is able.

Are we in need of a restored relationship? He is able to do more. Do we need a physical healing in our bodies? He is able to do more than we can imagine. Is there a financial lack in our lives? God is able to open the windows of heaven over us. Are we seeking direction or wisdom? He is able to give us more than we are asking for. Are we asking Him for business success, in order to funnel more resources into the kingdom of God? He is able to prosper us in all that we do. Are we pastoring a church and desiring to see it grow and make an impact in our community? Has God put a nation on our hearts and we are dreaming of ways to touch that land? Not only is nothing too hard for Him, but He is able to do more than we think He can. He is able to accomplish more in us and for us than we can even imagine.

The One who is at work in us, who is He? Who is this God in whom we are placing our faith? This is the Most High God, the Lord Jesus Christ. We can put our trust in Him. Make Him big. Exalt Him. Magnify the Lord. Let our faith soar to new levels. Run our race without getting weary. Fly on the wings of eagles. March into battle with a song. Get out of our boat and walk on water. Sing praises and start earthquakes. Send handkerchiefs to the sick. Shake off the snakes that have fastened themselves to our hands. Let all the doors be opened and everyone's chains be loosed. Break out of all limitation and be the people God originally intended us to be. He is able to keep us from falling and do far beyond what we can ask or think.

We do not let enemies, mountains, set backs, stumbling blocks, or unbelieving people stop us from believing that with God all things are possible. There is nothing too hard for the Lord our God, and with Him all things will work together for our good. He will lift up our head and encourage our heart, enlighten our eyes and set a plain path before us, making a way where there was no way.

We have nations to influence, churches to build, businesses to start, careers to launch, prayers to pray, and miracles to perform. We *"can do all things through Christ who strengthens"*[29] us. We can grow from faith to faith. We can believe. We can see miracles. As we make God big in our lives, we can be a person of great faith!

HE IS THE ALPHA AND OMEGA

Behold He comes with clouds and every eye will see Him and those also who pierced Him. He comes with ten thousand of His saints. He will be revealed from heaven with His mighty angels, with flaming fire taking vengeance on those who do not know God or obey the Gospel of our Lord Jesus Christ. He will come in that day to be glorified in His saints and to be admired among all those who believe.

He is the First and the Last, the Amen, the Last Adam. He is the One who was, who is, and who is to come. He it is who was dead but now is alive forevermore. He is the One who walks among the golden candlesticks. He is the Angel and Messenger to the Churches. He is coming to judge the earth. He will judge the world with righteousness and the peoples with truth.

He is the Judge of the living and the dead, the Judge of the whole earth, the Lawgiver. He is Melchizedek, King of Salem, King of Peace. He is the Wonderful Counselor, the Everlasting Father, and the Prince of

Peace. He is the Ancient of Days, the Apostle and High Priest of our con-fession—the Commander of heaven's armies. He is the Brightness of His glory, the Bright and Morning Star, the DayStar, the Dayspring from on high, the Desire of all nations. He is the heavenly Bridegroom, and the Fairest of Ten Thousand.

He is El Shaddai—God Almighty; the God of the whole earth; the God who alone is wise, who does wonders; the Great God; the Great King above all gods; the Great King over all the earth; the King of Kings and Lord of Lords. He is the King eternal, immortal, invisible; the Blessed and only Potentate. He is the One who inhabits eternity, the Governor, the One who has the keys of Hades and Death.

He is the Head of the Church; the Heir of all things; the High and Lofty One whose Name is Faithful and True. This is He who loved us and washed us from our sins, who rides on the clouds, who rides on the heaven of heavens. He is the Horn of my salvation. He is the Lamb of God who takes away the sin of the world, and He is the Lion of the Tribe of Judah who alone is worthy to open the seals and read the scrolls of God. He is the Lord on High, the Majesty on high, and the Messiah.

He is the Reaper, the Root and Offspring of David, the Ruler over the kings of the earth, our Scepter. He is the Seed of the woman, destined to crush the head of the dragon and rule the nations with a rod of iron. He is our Sure Foundation and our Dwelling Place in all generations. He knows the end from the beginning. He started a good work in us and will complete it until the day of Christ.

He who overcomes shall inherit all things, and I will be his God and he shall be My son. I am the Alpha and the Omega, the Beginning and the End, the First and the Last. I, Jesus, have sent My angel to testify to you these things in the churches. I am the Root and the Offspring of David, the Bright and Morning Star.

And the Spirit and the bride say, "Come!" And let him who hears say, "Come!" He who testifies to these things says, "Surely I am coming quickly." Amen. Even so, come, Lord Jesus!

NOTES

CHAPTER ONE

1 Matthew 13:44
2 Matthew 13:45-46
3 Romans 10:17
4 Romans 8:14
5 John 10:4
6 Isaiah 45:2
7 Ephesians 3:20

CHAPTER TWO

1 Matthew 14:31
2 Psalm 34:3
3 Isaiah 10:27
4 Psalm 23:4
5 Psalm 34:3
6 Deuteronomy 6:12
7 Joshua 5:15
8 Psalm 68:5
9 Isaiah 54:5
10 Psalm 77:14
11 Psalm 103:3
12 Psalm 71:6
13 Proverbs 15:29
14 Psalm 43:4
15 Psalm 119:114
16 Psalm 18:2
17 Psalm 121:5
18 Psalm 18:2
19 Psalm 3:3
20 Psalm 27:1
21 Psalm 73:26
22 Psalm 19:14

23 Psalm 71:7
24 Psalm 24:8
25 Psalm 93:4
26 Psalm 95:6
27 Psalm 134:3
28 Psalm 18:46
29 Psalm 121:5
30 Psalm 80:1
31 Psalm 3:3
32 Psalm 73:26
33 Psalm 18:2
34 Psalm 84:11
35 Psalm 46:1
36 Isaiah 54:10
37 Isaiah 49:7
38 Isaiah 43:16
39 Isaiah 57:15
40 Revelation 22:13
41 Revelation 1:18
42 Revelation 1:18
43 John 6:35
44 John 10:9
45 John 10:14
46 John 8:12
47 John 11:25
48 John 15:5
49 John 14:6
50 Revelation 22:12
51 Hebrews 3:1
52 1 Peter 2:7
53 1 Peter 2:7-8
54 1 Timothy 2:5
55 Psalm 22:3

NOTES

⁵⁶ John 4:23
⁵⁷ Psalm 34:1

CHAPTER THREE

¹ Judges 7:20
² John 2:5

CHAPTER FOUR

¹ Luke 6:38
² Ephesians 3:20
³ 2 Corinthians 5:21

CHAPTER FIVE

¹ Mark 11:22
² John 3:16
³ Matthew 15:26-28
⁴ Luke 18:8
⁵ 2 Chronicles 16:9
⁶ John 4:24
⁷ Mark 4:38-40
⁸ Romans 10:17
⁹ Exodus 15:26
¹⁰ Romans 10:10
¹¹ Proverbs 3:5
¹² Psalm 27:5
¹³ John 20:29
¹⁴ 1 Timothy 1:17
¹⁵ Proverbs 29:25
¹⁶ Matthew 14:29
¹⁷ Ephesians 6:13
¹⁸ Matthew 28:18-19
¹⁹ Genesis 15:5

CHAPTER SIX

¹ Romans 10:17
² Romans 8:28
³ Psalm 84:11
⁴ John 14:6
⁵ Acts 8:26-38
⁶ Romans 1:17
⁷ Mark 9:22-24
⁸ 2 Peter 3:18
⁹ Matthew 19:14

CHAPTER SEVEN

¹ Numbers 13:33
² Psalm 23:4
³ Matthew 14:31
⁴ James 1:22
⁵ 1 Corinthians 8:1
⁶ Ephesians 6:12
⁷ Matthew 15:13-14

CHAPTER EIGHT

¹ Matthew 12:34
² Proverbs 23:7
³ Proverbs 3:5
⁴ Romans 12:2
⁵ Ephesians 4:23
⁶ Romans 1:21
⁷ Proverbs 4:23
⁸ Philippians 4:6-7
⁹ Hebrews 3:13
¹⁰ Psalms 78:9
¹¹ Romans 14:23